The Game Is Rigged.

How to profit from the coming global economic collapse.

By Gregory J. Mannarino.

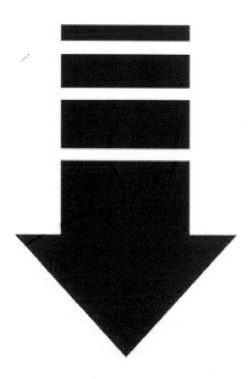

**Content includes never before published information on the world's next SUPER bubble!

The Game is Rigged.

How to profit from the coming global economic collapse.

by

Gregory J Mannarino.

Copyright 2011 by Gregory J. Mannarino

ISBN: 978-1-105-37317-6

Contents.

Introduction.

Bar none the U.S. economy is the biggest rigged game in the history of the world.

I should know, as the saying goes
"it takes one to know one."

Hello, my name is Gregory Mannarino and I am the author of The Gregorian Strategy for Multiple Deck Blackjack, Lyle Stuart 2002. That book included the first and only basic strategy system designed to be played against multiple deck casino blackjack games.

I have been engaged with gaming on a professional level since the early 1990's. I also worked on Wall Street as an independent trader from the mid 1990's through the early 2000's. I hold a medical degree and practice clinical medicine in Las Vegas Nevada where I live. As an undergraduate I studied finance, economics, and natural sciences. I served as a commissioned officer in the United States Naval Reserve Medical Service Corps, having attained the rank of lieutenant. And as a hobby I enjoy studying military tactics and strategy.

Having been profoundly involved with the gaming industry, Wall Street trading, my penchant for economics, finance, and military tactics, has provided me with a unique and compelling perspective into the machinations involved.

For me understanding what makes something tick has always been fascinating. Human behavior as well.

Human psychology plays an enormous role in gaming as well as economics. In fact what most people fail to realize is that consumer sentiment, which is the commonly used term for consumer "psyche," is the main driver involved in equity trading as well as economics. Fundamental or technical factors involving the overall markets play a back seat role to human perception in determining an asset's price, where the overall market is headed, and whether an economy thrives or collapses.

The science of economics is not a straight forward idea, and in many ways it is like the practice of medicine in that the expected outcome my be different than the actual result.

Economies or more specifically how an economy is run is massively influenced by human conceptualization, and today more than any other time history with the merger of government and corporate entity's here in the United States perception by the American people is everything.

My purpose in writing this book is not to bury you with statistics and numbers with multiple zeros behind them so you can go ooh and ah while at the same time filling up blank pieces of paper. All of the numbers and statistics involved are easily discoverable and can be found in virtually all of the other books written involving the understanding of our economy.

My point here is to try and raise people's awareness as to the human side of this super game.

Question: why is it so important to know how to play this game?

Answer: because every citizen of every country in the world is forced to participate in this game, and play it.

This is no ordinary Las Vegas casino where all you can lose is your money no, in this global casino people are losing their lives. At this point in time on every corner of the world we are witnessing increasing social unrest and political strife. These things are not only going to be growing much worse in their scope, size, and in their violence over the next few years, but they are coming right to your front door.

There is great change taking place everywhere in the world, and an enormous amount of effort is being put into causing the people of the western world to believe they are isolated from these problems. Not only is this a complete falsehood, but in my opinion it is criminal for those who have been voted into office by the American people and have had our trust placed in them to go along with this charade, for they are well aware that a monster is headed our way.

A financial wave of destruction is coming which is going to shake the foundation of our beloved country the likes of which nightmares could not even duplicate. Still where is their warning?

It would seem that our policymakers are naive to all this, however they are fully cognizant of these things . It would also seem that our policymakers are just overly concerned with staying in office, but this as well is not what it seems. For some the root cause of these things remains elusive, but there is only one clear answer.

Here is where this all begins.
This macroeconomic super game for which you are a direct participant has rules, and I am going to explain clearly what the rules are. I will detail for you where the dangers lie, and I will show you who the major players are. But most importantly I am going to teach you how to win.
It must be understood that you cannot win this game by beating the major players of which there are three, as they cannot be beaten.

11.

The only way you can win this game is by having a clear understanding of how this game is going to play out, and that is the sole reason why I wrote this book.

I suppose the real question is this, are you willing to fight for your life? Your survival is on the line in this game, so I hope you have got what it takes to win. You can think of this book as a survival manual.

In any game, project, investment, etc. you cannot simply "fly by the seat of your pants" so to speak and just hope for the best. Understand that there are people on the other side of the equation who are hoping you do just that. You have to be aware of how decisions you make at any given moment are going to affect you in the long run. Too many people just live in the moment, which is nice for that brief period of time, but you have to understand the ramifications of your actions, or inaction's for that matter. Newtons 3rd physical law dictates: *every action has an equal and opposite reaction.* But what would happen if inaction from an animate being leads to misfortune?

Does that mean that an action had actually taken place? Sir Newton seems to suggest that inaction would have no reaction, so are Human beings immune from physical laws? More on this concept later on.

Understanding the game.

This economic super game is global, but because the United States is the biggest economy of them all most of the rules begin here. In the course of events, by the time most people figure out what is going on it is already way too late. A vast majority of the time when the general public acts on a opportunity the situation has already played out or is close to conclusion. This scenario has been repeated countless times throughout history. How many times have you heard someone say, "wow I wish I would have got in on that sooner, I would be rich today." Or how about this: I bought my house at the market peak, and now the value of my house has plummeted.

What I want to convey to you is a sense of urgency. We are at a precipice, a major economic tectonic shift of epic proportions is just beyond the horizon and there is no way to stop it from coming right at you. The urgency is this: you can choose to survive it or not. It is my hope that you choose to survive.

Please do not misunderstand me, this macroeconomic monster which is evolving as you are reading this sentence is going to unleash horror upon the human race, and in several parts of the world it has already begun.

Today right in the midst of this developing global economic crisis, in direct response to it point of fact, there is an opportunity for people to become massively wealthy. The vast majority of the general population of not just the United States, but the world are going to be left destitute, and many will continue to die. But some like you, simply because you are reading this book right now have the opportunity of a lifetime.

Throughout history it is at times like these when fortunes are made, and also lost.

Before we really get going. In order to understand how things work in this super game we are going to have to learn a little bit more about ourselves, what drives us, what influences our thoughts and actions, and how these mechanisms will determine who will come out of this thing we are all going to witness unscathed, much the better, or not at all.

Regardless of what you may believe at this moment your very behavior, in fact in many ways the person you are right now has been "caused to happen." For example: let's say you were born in a part of the world with little or no exposure to a television, advertisements, or education. Or perhaps reared in a nomadic African tribe, or brought up by wolves. Do you think you would be the same person you are now? Dress the same? Act the same? Think the same thoughts?

The social structure we live in and adapt to as a whole decides who and what you are to a great extent.

Here in the United States we have information overload to the nth degree, and not all of this information is there to help you to succeed, in fact a great deal of the information is distributed with the intent to cause you to fail.

Let me ask you, how is it that throughout history certain individuals were able to persuade throngs of people to follow them? To do things they knew in their hearts was morally wrong? What causes us to act in a specific manner or make us go this way when we just could have easily gone the other?

In order to understand what causes us to do "this instead of that" we are going to need answers to these questions, and we will do just that throughout this book.

The decisions we make with regard to what we purchase, how we invest, how we raise our families, etc. are heavily influenced by "invisible factors." There are also "ominous factors," things which through the disbursement of misinformation cause a change in perception and as such influence the decisions we make to the benefit of others.

As an example of how some of these "factors" work, let me speak briefly about my first book. That book included a new basic strategy system which took into account the evolution of the game of blackjack. The most basic changes was moving from one deck used in play, to multiple decks shuffled together. I also took into consideration how the rules for the game had also changed over time. What I would consider to be an "invisible factor" with regard to this game is this: as the deck's of cards are played out during the game, each card taken out of play changes the overall composition of the deck, therefore a "perfect strategy" would have to take this into account.

Being that most of the cards in blackjack have a value of 10, *and this is especially true for the multiple deck games,* as the game progresses it is much more beneficial for the player to "hit" on hands that he would never consider hitting on in a single deck game. And it worked! I consider this an "invisible factor" simply because the average player would not think about the composition of the deck changing as the game is played out. The invisible factors involved in either a blackjack game, or anything else weigh heavily on who wins and who loses. This is why being educated with regard to any undertaking is critical, as these "invisible factors" can and will eat you alive.

The "ominous factors" involved with regard to my effective system of blackjack was the misinformation which I believe was being put out by the casinos regarding my strategy. My system worked hands down and I made a small fortune using it at the time, and so did many of my readers, but then something very interesting happened.

I started getting letters and emails from people who had been using my system saying it was becoming very hard for them to find games meeting the criteria I describe in my book. In direct response to my new blackjack strategy the casinos changed the rules for the game!

Today it is very difficult to find a game in which a "blackjack" pays 3:2; most games since the publication of my strategy now pay just 6:5 for a "blackjack." Not only did my strategy cause the casinos to make this one major change, it also forced them to alter the rules regarding splitting cards and what hands could be doubled down on. Admittedly the changes instituted by the casinos effectively killed the game. I suppose in some ways it could be said that my blackjack book was a milestone book, in that only one time before in gaming history were the rules for a modern casino game changed because of a new strategy for the game of blackjack. Today the game of blackjack now is unbeatable over the long run no matter what system you may choose to use. The fact that the game was beatable at one time is what drew people to the game.

19.

My first book is out of print now and originally sold for around 12 bucks. If you were to go on Amazon right now and try to get one, an unread copy is going for somewhere around a hundred bucks! Wow, who knew? Ironically I don't even have a copy for myself anymore as I gave them all away.

There is another way which the "ominous factors" can work against you. The first one I spoke about was by the proliferation of misinformation, and the second is by withholding information. Each of these is equally deceptive.

The invisible factors come about simply by not being aware, the ominous factors are meant to deliberately mislead whether by inclusion of the wrong information or excluding the right information. By having an understanding of the "invisible" factors, it is exceedingly difficult to be deceived by the "ominous" factors which brings us full circle. Educate yourself about whatever you choose, or choose not to do, and you will always be the better for it.

Take no prisoners.

This economic super game is as close to a winner takes all that I have ever come to know, and in order to play this mega game out to conclusion you have to understand the parameters. In fact this economic/political game is being played with stakes so high it has the potential to wipe out the lives, in the literal sense, of most of the worlds population and we are witnessing the beginnings of that now.

The rules? Yes this game has rules just like the game blackjack does, and these rules are not the same for everyone.

Its not just about Wall Street.

I empathize with the Occupy Wall Street Movement however, their efforts in my opinion are somewhat misdirected. It seems that a lot of their discontent is over there being such a great gap between those that have, and those that have a lot less.

The problem I have with this thought process is this: an almost total misunderstanding of how it got this way, and it got that way not by Wall Street but by Main Street. It was the perception that the party would never end of those on Main Street which drove the massive real estate/housing bubble, and it was the popping of the housing bubble which is the root cause for a great deal of today's economic woes in the U.S. In fact more than likely it was the parents of those involved in OWS who helped drive the stock market and the real estate markets to unsustainable levels leading to their collapse. Oh you would never, ever, hear a policymaker say such a thing, but it is the plain, hard, cold, truth.

What OWS should be concerned about is not where we have been, but where we are going regarding the Federal Reserves unrelenting attack on the American people as a whole by continuing to destroy the value of the dollar and crushing savers offering then negative returns on their interest earning accounts.

Earlier I elaborated on how the general public tends to take advantage of an opportunity too late, well here, even if OWS continues to grow it is way too late. The plain truth is we have already hit a critical mass with regard to the financial/economic meltdown hurling our way. What those in the OWS movement should be doing is preparing for what is to come.

What is important for people to realize is that the investment banks and those who's anger is being directed at by OWS could not possibly care less if we are in either an economic boom or a depression headed for a collapse. All they are concerned with is how to capitalize on the situation. We as individuals are like insects to them and honestly you should be OK with that and I will tell you why. All of this presents us, you and me, with unprecedented opportunity.

For those on the inside this is like the goose which lays the golden eggs. An opportunity like this is a once in a lifetime thing so don't be upset, you are learning how to make it all work for you here with this book.

23.

I will tell you something else, the investment banks and major corporations which are two parts of the same thing, along with policymakers as well, do not care where the economy as a whole is going. They are for the most part, *as there are a few policymakers who do care*, a group which I like to call collectively the "politicocorporatists." The politicocorporatists represent the merger between the policymakers and the corporate powers. In using the term corporate powers again, I am encompassing the major corporations and the investment banks. The people who are responsible for the operations of these companies have one thing in mind, and that is their own interests and that of their families and why? Because they are well aware that the endgame is at hand. Unless you are an insider within that said company, meaning a member of the board or a major shareholder your interests simply do not matter.

Today on a global level we are witnessing a phenomenon, a truly epic unfolding of events the likes of which have never been seen or witnessed before in human history. However most people have no idea what is happening or how these events are going to affect them. I am not just talking about your average Joe here. I am talking about highly educated people, money managers, and investors. There are so many factors at play from deliberate market manipulation to outright lies about some kind of economic recovery that by far the vast majority of the American people simply have no clue as to what is going to befall them, and even less of an idea of how to capitalize from it. For most people it is just like noise, hard to interpret, difficult to understand, and this is a product of how they are deliberately being made to feel. Today it is very difficult for the average person to simply carry out a typical day. We get up early, get dressed, go to work where we have to deal with 8+ hours of stress, then come home exhausted, go to sleep, and repeat the same thing day after day, year after year. Yes it is extremely difficult to do all these things while at the same time paying attention to this thing, or that thing.

What ends up happening is peoples brain stops functioning normally and falls into a rhythm, or pattern, and blocks out almost everything else, it is a self preservation defense mechanism. In my professional medical opinion the typical, pattern type, incredibly stressful lifestyle the vast majority of us are forced to live is the leading cause for disease bar none. When I was in school studying medicine I had to write a paper outlining the effects of stress on the body's immune system, the results are conclusive. When the body undergoes stress, the adrenal cortex releases cortisol. Cortisol is a natural steroid, when released in the body it causes several things to happen, one of which is a suppression of the body's immune system. The suppression of the body's immune system leaves the body open to attack by bacteria, viruses, fungi, and all manner or micro-organism causing various diseases. Prolonged exposure to stress, the kind you would expect as a by product of living a stressful/average lifestyle and thus having excess corticosteroid within the body not only leads to increased risk of infections caused by microbes, but stroke, heart attack, hypertension, cancer, obesity, mental disorders, and premature death. All of this is documented medical fact.

.

In the medical science of psychology there is a condition known as "a normalcy bias." A normalcy bias can cause a rational person to reject the blatantly obvious. The fear of change, even if that change could save that persons life is dismissed by the individual or even in some cases masses of people who may be drawn into a situation which seems impossible or farfetched. Those who are affected with a normalcy bias tend to say things like, "something like that has never happened here before, so I just don't believe it will ever happen." You can easily foresee the possible ramifications of this type of thought process.

I do not wish to downplay the severity of the crisis which is unfolding, apocalyptic would be a better word to describe what I and many others with a clear understanding of how this game is going to play out foresee occurring.

The biggest mistake which any person can make is to underestimate the severity of a given situation. Many battles and total wars have been lost because of underestimation. Underestimating has caused many a nation to collapse, corporations to lose market share, business to fail, investments to suffer, and people to die, among other things as well.

It is always better to over prepare, because being unprepared when a crisis hits almost always leads to utter failure.

Sun Tzu the Art of War tells us that its is always better to have the high ground, and to be first on the field of battle.

Section 1.
We are not all drinking the same Kool-Aid.

The first thing to be absolutely sure of if this: the rules for this game are not standardized, they are vastly different favoring some over others. In gaming terms the deck is stacked against you. Who are the main players of this game, simple: the White House and Wall Street, the politicocorporatists. To narrow this down even further we can safely say the policymakers in Washington and the investment banks. These two entities in every sense are in bed together, in fact today they can be regarded as one and the same. They are equal participants in a "super" game in which their can be only one conclusion. There is in fact one more major player in this game however for now let's just focus on these two. I will tell you who the third prime player is later on in section 2.

With a show of hands, how many of you believe that with regard to trading stock XYZ you are privy to the same information say the CEO of Goldman Sachs is?

Or on issues of policy's or upcoming laws and regulations you have the same knowledge as a congressman? Or if you decide to trade commodities, you are made aware before time of an upcoming margin change requirement? It goes on and on and on. And here is where is gets even better, not only do those on the inside act upon information that you and I are not privy to and get handsomely reward financially, they are not prosecuted. In fact if you are a member of congress it's actually legal for you to act on non-public information.

Below is an excerpt which was taken from the Wall Street Journal, (WSJ) 11-16-11.

To the extent our legislators are trading on their own unique political knowledge, at least they are thinking about the impact of their policies on productive businesses. To the extent they make a quick profit, at least they are paying the top personal tax rate, so helping to finance the spending they inflict on the rest of us. After all, the real scandal isn't what they do with their own money, but what they do with ours.

The free market is dead.

OK. So we are now beginning to understand that the game is rigged, now what. Well, what else do we know? We absolutely know the free market is dead. Therefore a whole new set of rules exist.

Free market is dead? Yes, stone cold dead in fact. From the time the government decided to institute the Troubled Asset Relief Program, (TARP), under then president Bush the free market was dead. In a free market those who have made bad bets are supposed to fail, it is the most basic principal in a free capitalistic society. No where in the constitution of the United States is there such a provision where the public is supposed to bail out failing corporations and or individuals for that matter. The writers of the constitution warned against such measures. Not only did the free market essentially die, a whole new form of government was instituted. We now have a corporate state controlled by the government, aka the policymakers and the investment banks and as such the politicocorporatists were created. I will go one step further.

The terrorist attacks of September 11, 2001 presented an unprecedented opportunity to those who were seeking to usurp the government of the United States. They succeeded.

So yes the rules have changed. Not only have the rules been altered greatly skewing the odds in the favor of the well informed, but the playing field itself has also changed dramatically.

In the equity markets of today fifty percent of market action is High Frequency Trading, and HFT adds massive liquidity to the markets. Well financed players can and do take advantage of this mode, (HFT), of trading by deliberately manipulating the price of equities through collusion. It is very difficult for market oversight to recognize collusion with HFT because of 2 factors. The first is the modality of HFT itself it is very complex and mostly run by computer programs, and the second is High Frequency **Trades themselves** take advantage of extremely brief moments of change in an assets price and some of these changes are deliberately caused to happen.

The manipulation of market price of just about anything can and is done quite simply and rather frequently. Central banks manipulate asset prices all the time, one of the many ways in which they do it is with something called Gold Swaps.

Using gold swaps, world central banks can pass, or "swap," large amounts of gold for foreign currency or other assets either between each other or foreign governments. The effect of these transactions is simple, market manipulation in either the price of gold, currency exchange rates, etc. These "swaps" are fostered through what is known as the BIS which is an abbreviation for Bank for Internal Settlements. The BIS is the world's central banks, bank. In 1944 the Czech Republic accused the BIS of laundering gold which was stolen by the Nazi's during their blitz through Europe.

The BIS states that it, along with the world's central banks maintain international financial stability. I call it "influencing the world markets for the benefit the central bankers." The BIS is self governed, is under no countries jurisdiction, and does not answer to anyone. The BIS along with the worlds central banks can manipulate and twist the world markets however they please at any time they want.

Currency values are highly manipulated as well, For example: the Chinese buy American dollars in order to manipulate exchange rates so they can keep the value of the dollar high in relation to the Yuan. This is done to assure that Chinese exports are kept "cheap." In fact the Chinese hold the largest reserves of foreign currency in the world for this very reason, to manipulate currency rates. The Chinese know how to play the game, in fact they make the rules when it comes to currency trading.

Basic economics tells us that an assets price is driven by supply and demand. While supply and demand drivers are responsible to a certain degree with regard to the market price of an item, the main price driver of a given entity is psychological, driven by fear and greed. More on this later on but for now it is important to keep in mind that the price of any trade-able item can and is easily manipulated to illicit a specific response.

In fact today so much market activity is manipulated in some way it is hard to discern reality from fantasy.

Running a close second to China with regard to market manipulation is The Federal Reserve however, a more likely scenario is they are both equally guilty of tremendous amounts of market manipulation spanning the gamut.

With regard to the rhetoric coming from the politicocorporatists and parroted by the mass media let's start with this. There is no real market/economic recovery. None, zero, zilch.

In fact there will not be any real recovery until the overall markets are allowed to correct. The Fed has been manipulating the U.S. Markets extensively since the housing price correction/stock market correction began, however due to direct intervention/manipulation the correction was not allowed to play out to conclusion. The politicocorporatists started it all with the "too big to fails."

Please allow me elaborate on the most powerful and effective manipulation method known to and by man, its called **fear**. If you can cause people to have fear you can control and manipulate their behavior. It is very simple and totally effective.

Every day we are bombarded with adds, television commercials, all manner of devices which attempt to cause us to favor this product over that, or do this and not that, etc, etc.
Governments take this to the extreme and instill fear into the mass public to cause their desired effect. To further illustrate how the institution of fear is utilized by

government upon its people here is a quote I would like you to read and consider:

"naturally, the common people don't want war; neither in Russia nor in England nor in America, nor for that matter in Germany. That is understood. But, after all, it is the leaders of the country who determine the policy and it is always a simple matter to drag the people along, whether it is a democracy or a fascist dictatorship or a Parliament or a Communist dictatorship."

That quote was from Herman Goring who knew a little about how governments deliberately manipulate human behavior. Herman Goring was a leading member of the Nazi party, and was Commander in Chief of the German air force during World War II. He was second in command only to Adolf Hitler himself.

Carter G. Woodson, who was an American historian, educator, and author, had this to say: *"if you can control a man's thinking you do not have to worry about his action. When you determine what a man shall think you do not have to concern yourself about what he will do."*

It is also important to keep in mind that having control of the information dispersed to the masses through media outlets is of critical importance. Keeping people distracted through the use of the mass media is very decisive tool. Up until the last days of WWII the German people believed that they were winning the war because that is what the media was telling them.

Simple economics would also have us believe that there are cycles in all economies, meaning that is there are up cycles followed by down cycles and so on. What is occurring now in America is not anywhere near or like a simple economic down cycle. If we were in a simple downward economic cycle as they would have us believe, the Fed would not be trying so desperately to manipulate the overall market. The truth is the Fed is in panic mode and the same is true for all the world's central banks.

Let's talk more about there being no real recovery.
Prior to the Fed's (quantitative easing) QE1, also known
as money printed out of thin air, the stock market had
corrected nearly 50 percent and housing was in also in a
downward spiral. Then like magic the Fed initiated QE
and poof! The market began to rebound and the falling
housing prices slowed. Then QE ended. What happened
next?

The equity markets began to fall and housing again
began to speed its downward trajectory. No worries, here
comes QE2 and again poof! The overall markets
improved. Then when QE2 ended markets again began
to falter and the Fed initiated operation twist. In the midst
of all this the Fed has been keeping interest rates at
historic and artificial lows. In a statement made by Fed
Chairman Ben Bernanke during one of his meetings he
states "the Fed will keep interest rates low through 2013.
But wait, QE2 was supposed to have ended. Without
overtly admitting it, the Fed just initiated QE3.

Understand: the Fed can't just go ahead and "say" we are continuing to keep interest rates low, it has to actually get into the market and make it happen.

In this case the Fed is continuing to buy long term bonds with money printed out of thin air and will continue to do so until at least 2013.

All this market manipulation by the Fed gives the illusion of some type of economic recovery, but it is simply not there. Housing has not recovered, in fact it will continue to fall, and unemployment despite all the governments' efforts continues to be high.

The stock market loves all this cheap money being printed by the Fed rebounding from a low of around 6,500 but as soon as the fruit punch is taken away it too will drop.

The reasons why both the real estate market and the stock market have to resume their downward trajectory are two fold.

First: market forces were and are continuing to be artificially manipulated to cause them to rebound, and second: the fundamental reasons why they were falling still exist.

In a healthy economy yes, market cycles do exist, but today we have anything but a healthy economy that is just in a normal economic downturn.

All the parameters have changed dramatically, and will continue to do so.

It must be understood that the main drivers of our economy are gone and will not return for decades if ever. The economy of the United States is driven by consumer spending, in fact seventy percent of it. During the housing boom, right up until its inevitable collapse our economy and our markets were the envy of the world. It was simple greed which drove this economic engine at an unsustainable rate. The meteoric rise in the price of housing and other real estate assets in the United States was driven by the factor of greed fueled by cheap available money.

The rise in real estate assets was disproportionate with incomes and economic growth, and any liability which continues to rise in this manner is in a bubble, and all economic bubbles pop there are no exceptions.

During this time of prosperity people spent money on everything in excess. Unemployment was low and people were making money. Even so, many people used their appreciating real estate assets as banks drawing on its increasing value which seemed like it would never end. Banks were giving out mortgages to everyone and anyone like candy. Many of these people were sub-prime but the banks didn't care and neither did the people buying these homes. Many of the people had no interest in keeping the homes and simply wanted to flip the home and turn a quick profit. So the terms of these loans didn't matter either. No one, obviously not even the people making these loans, ever thought the party would end. Rising real estate values were here to stay! Just didn't turn out that way. Therefore since the popping of the housing bubble, all the rules have changed.

With the popping of the housing bubble poof! There goes the main driver of consumer spending. The rise of the housing bubble which was the main driver of economic growth since the 1980's is gone. The epic rise of real estate values along with the massive consumer spending driven by that rise had paved the way for businesses to thrive and jobs to be created. All of that is finished, totally played out. Therefore without that main driver of economic growth whatever the Fed tries to do or grandstanding by President Obama nothing can bring it back. The jobs which were lost during the deflating of the housing bubble are not coming back.

The divers of a healthy economy simply in a downturn do not exist anymore, instead what we have is a perfect storm which has not even come close to its full devastating power yet. We are in for far more that a prolonged "depression," we are just about staring into a financial abyss. However, it is at times like this that fortunes will be made for some, that is if you know how to play the game.

Some people may argue that there has been a rise in gross domestic product (GDP) since the, laugh out loud, end of the great recession. I would say really? And here is why: never before in the history of the United States has there been such enormous government spending during a "downward economic cycle," which adds to GDP. If you were to calculate out the immense spending the government has done attempting to pump up our dying economy, which would include money printed out of thin air by the Fed to purchase long term bonds, (by the way so far the Fed has increased the money supply over three hundred percent and counting since 2008), you would get negative GDP, no growth. In fact you would have contraction.

The Bigger They Are The Harder They Fall.
Having an understanding of the game rules makes it easy to play and win. They say a picture is worth a thousand words so let's look at some charts.

Take a look at this chart.

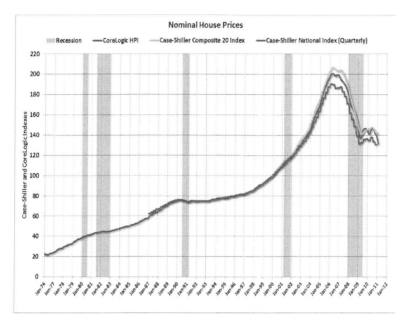

This chart above demonstrates a clear bubble pattern, in this case the housing bubble.

What can also be gleaned from this chart is clearly real estate prices have a lot more to fall, (more on this later).

Right now housing prices seem to have slowed and in some parts of the country have even begin to rise however, this is solely due to intervention from the Fed and not due to any positive fundamentals within the real estate market. If anything the fundamentals within the real estate market are still deteriorating.

The current Federal Reserves economic policy's are not only destined to fail for many reasons which will be discussed throughout this book, but are actually making the long term problems much worse, devastatingly so actually.

Its all about fair market value.
It must be understood that all market forces seek one thing, and that is fair market value, that is their sole job if you will. All the collusion, market manipulation by the Fed, etc. etc. has to fail over time because the market forces are enormous, way bigger that any entity'(s) efforts to control it.

At this point in time because of the continuing market manipulation by the Fed the worlds biggest bubble is being created, a super mega bubble, and when this bubble pops which is something we are starting to already see in Europe every remaining economic bubble which still exist not just only here in the United States but globally are going to tumble until they over-correct. This something we will discuss later on in section 4.

It is unfortunate that government and non-government entities, (the Fed and the other world central banks), believe that they can control the markets. Because of this people around the globe are going to suffer greatly.

Let's look at this another way. The ratio of investors world wide to central bankers is about 10,000 to 1, yet the central bankers believe that they which represent a fraction of a percent know better how to "run the markets" better than the vast majority. They have refused to allow natural market dynamics/a free market to determine fair asset values, so they, the vast minority solely because they have the power to do so keep acting upon the markets unnaturally and unilaterally.

This repeated and direct market intervention is going to lead to financial devastation across the board sometime in the near future and here is why: before market dynamics force themselves into correction, the central banks of the world are going to continue to pump up the markets with the printing of massive amounts of fiat money. This type of intervention is going to compound the problem exponentially. In fact they are going to try and come up with and impose any and every conceivable scheme ever devised in trying to push off the popping of this mega bubble, but when the eventual forced market correction occurs at that point the ramifications are going to shake the world.

Understand, the only way they can push off the inevitable collapse is to compound the root cause of the problem, excessive and massive debt. Its like trying to save a drowning man by throwing more water on him.

Take a look at the chart of the DOW below.

If you look at this chart and the previous chart of the housing index it is clear that the housing boom fueled the subsequent stock market boom. There is also a clear lag. The housing boom really got going in the 1980's, and this fueled consumer spending, created jobs, allowed businesses to grow, and then in the early 1990's caused the spike in the equity markets.

At the very moment real estate prices began to fall the equity markets followed suit, there was no lag time. This should demonstrate to you how important the relationship is between real estate and the equity market, and it should also demonstrate to you why the Federal Reserve is so "Hell Bent" on trying to pump up real estate values and not allowing them to correct to their fair market value. The Fed believes that by artificially stimulating businesses this will create jobs, while this policy may create some jobs in the short run as soon as the fruit punch is taken away poof! There goes those artificially created jobs. In order for there to be a sustained and "real" economic recovery substantial economic drivers need to be created. The Feds stimulus does not create economic drivers, it only creates an artificial environment across the board... And, more debt.

Section 2.
An Economy on Life Support.

The major players are surely aware of how this game is going to play out, make no mistake about that. Who are the major players again? Yes, the policymakers and the investment banks but we shall call them the politicocorporatists.

Let's explore the concept of the corporate elites being one and the same as the policymakers for a moment. Below I have included a list of several prior Goldman Sachs executives who currently or recently hold/held high positions in the U.S. Government:

Dianna Farrell: Obama Administration: Deputy Director, National Economic Council. Former Goldman Sachs Title: Financial Analyst.

Stephen Friedman: Obama Administration: Chairman, President's Foreign Intelligence Advisory Board. Former Goldman Sachs Title: Board Member (Chairman, 1990-94; Director, 2005-).

Gary Gensler: Obama Administration: Commissioner, Commodity Futures Trading Commission. Former Goldman Sachs Title: Partner and Co-head of Finance.

Robert Hormats: Obama Administration: Undersecretary for Economic, Energy and Agricultural Affairs, State Department. Former Goldman Sachs Title: Vice Chairman, Goldman Sachs Group.

Philip Murphy: Obama Administration: Ambassador to Germany. Former Goldman Sachs Title: Head of Goldman Sachs, Frankfurt.

Mark Patterson: Obama Administration: Chief of Staff to Treasury Secretary, Timothy Geitner. Former Goldman Sachs Title: Lobbyist 2005-2008; Vice President for Government Relations.

John Thain: Obama Administration: Advisor to Treasury Secretary, Timothy Geitner. Former Goldman Sachs Title: President and Chief Operating Officer (1999-2003).

Henry Paulson: Bush II Administration: Secretary, Treasury 2006 - 2009. Former Goldman Sachs Title: Chairman and CEO (1998-2006).

Neel Kashkari: Bush II Administration: Assistant Secretary for Financial Stability, Treasury (2008 – 2009). Former Goldman Sachs Title: Vice President, San Francisco; led Information Technology Security Investment Banking Practice.

Reuben Jeffery: Bush II Administration: Undersecretary for Economic, Energy and Agricultural Affairs, State Department (2007 –2009). Former Goldman Sachs Title: Managing Partner Parisuntil 2002 Security Investment Banking Practice.

Robert Steel: Bush II Administration: Under Secretary for Domestic Finance, Treasury, (2006 – 2008). Former Goldman Sachs Title: Vice Chairman – 2004.

Steve Shafran: Bush II Administration: Advisor on setting up TARP to Treasury Secretary, Henry Paulson 2008. Former Goldman Sachs Title: Private equity business in Asia until 2000.

Edward C. Forst: Bush II Administration: Advisor on setting up TARP to Treasury Secretary, Henry Paulson 2008. Former Goldman Sachs Title: Co-head of Goldman's investment management business.

Dan Jester: Bush II Administration: Advisor on setting up TARP to Treasury Secretary, Henry Paulson 2008. Former Goldman Sachs Title: Deputy CFO.

Kendrick R. Wilson III: Bush II Administration: Advisor on setting up TARP to Treasury Secretary, Henry Paulson 2008. Former Goldman Sachs Title: Chairman of Goldman's financial institutions groups.

Joshua Bolten: Bush II Administration: White House Chief of Staff (2006 – 2009). Former Goldman Sachs Title: Executive Director, Legal & Government Affairs (1994-99).

Gary Gensler: Bush II Administration: Undersecretary, Treasury (1999-2001) and Assistant Secretary, Treasury (1997-1999). Former Goldman Sachs Title: Partner and Co-head of Finance.

Robert Rubin: Bush II Administration: Secretary, Treasury 1995-1999. Former Goldman Sachs Title: Vice Chairman (1987-90).

Robert Zoellick: Bush II Administration: United States Trade Representative (2001-2005), Deputy Secretary of State (2005-2006), World Bank President (2007 -). Former Goldman Sachs Title: Vice Chairman, International (2006-07).

William C Dudley: NY Federal Reserve: Current President/CEO. Former Goldman Sachs Title: Partner and managing director – 2007.

Stephen Friedman: NY Federal Reserve: Former Chairman of the Board – 2009. Former Goldman Sachs Title: Board Member (Chairman, 1990-94).

So what is really going on here?
Clearly Wall Street insiders are deeply embedded and involved in establishing the rules of this economic super game. In fact with regard to the TARP program: then treasury secretary Henry Paulson under Bush

got congress to approve a seven hundred billion dollar payout using U.S. tax payer dollars for his Wall Street buddies, and how did he do it? He did it by telling congress and the American people if they decided not to do it America would collapse financially.

Paulson used the oldest and most effective trick in the book to get TARP passed, fear.

Would America have collapsed financially without the TARP program? Absolutely not. Well what would have happened? The bad investments made by the investment banks would have been written off as losses, or partial losses, bonuses for the executives of these corporations would have been a bit less although still in the multiple seven figure range. But then perhaps some fundamental changes to the way investment banks take unnecessary risks would have been implemented, and better business models would have emerged. Instead no changes were made, the public, you and me, now own tens of billions in toxic assets including bad mortgages which continue to deteriorate and will do so for the foreseeable future.

If congress had actually put the American people first and did not approve TARP yes, there would have been some temporary financial pain and economic slowing which would have in turn put pressure on congressional leaders who would be facing re-election.

However the policymakers could not allow their political contributors to suffer one iota of pain, so they gave it to you instead.

The major problem is this: because of the relationship between the policymakers and the investment banks, the commons which are you are me, are being prepared for the slaughter yet to come.

Understand this and I will elaborate more on this during section 4. A financial wrecking ball is aimed straight at your head, it is unstoppable and it is approaching fast. *Don't worry, I am going to teach you how not only how to remove the target from the middle of your forehead, but also how you are going to capitalize on this upcoming event big time!*

With the popping of the housing bubble and the refusal of the politicocorporatists to allow natural market dynamics to take effect and correct in a normal way, what is being created is a financial monster. In a free market natural forces drive and direct asset prices, therefore over valued assets correct downward and under priced assets correct upward.

What we have now is an equity market being pumped up by cheap money and a housing market not being allowed to normalize. We also have an overall fake economic recovery being artificially suspended for the same reasons.

Once the forces which are being used by the Fed in collusion with the investment banks are stopped either by themselves, or involuntary pushed upon them by the massive natural market dynamics which eventually will prevail its party over.

It is important to understand that natural market forces are enormous, and all this pumping up cannot be sustained by any means. At some point market dynamics will prevail and force a major corrective move.

Since 2008 the Fed has increased the money supply 300%. Just think about that for a moment, **the Federal Reserve in order to slow the drop of real estate values and pump up the equity markets has increased the money supply by three hundred percent.**

To get a visual on this, take a look at this chart below. This chart demonstrates what a 300% increase in the monetary base actually looks like.

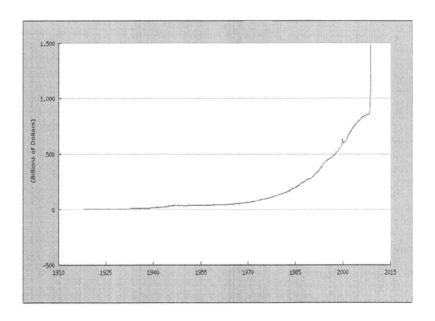

This chart above demonstrates the incredible parabolic move the monetary base has undergone since 2008 from the Fed literally printing money. Does this pattern look familiar to you? It is a classic bubble pattern and an economic bubble cannot be sustained. Look at the steady sloping increase in the monetary base from 1985 up to the parabolic move caused by the Fed's money printing, this was a natural increase in the money supply due to a booming economy.

The parabolic move as seen in the chart on the previous page is anything but natural or caused by a booming economy, or anything for that matter which may be seen in a typical economic slowdown during a healthy economy. It is unprecedented.

So from the information in the chart above it is clear that the Fed has the printing presses fired up and running on mega overdrive. So what's the problem some people have asked me?

The main problem is this: each dollar magically added to the monetary base by the Federal Reserve devalues each dollar already in circulation. That means that not in essence but in reality each day Ben Bernanke runs his printing press you are getting poorer. In fact ever since Ben pushed the panic button and cranked up his printing presses in 2008 your dollar has lost 15 percent of its value.

Lets look at this another way. Lets say you have ten grand stuffed under your mattress, that ten grand will buy you the equivalent of eighty five hundred dollars worth of the same goods in today's money. Old Ben is attacking you directly and financially more and more each and every day by running his printing presses in hyper mode.

.

The Federal Reserve's current policies of devaluing the dollar more and more by printing epic sums of money out of thin air is robbing the American people, rich and poor alike, by taking away the purchasing power of our money. However, there is a simple strategy that counters this move, and I will elaborate on this at length in section 5.

Please keep in mind, and this goes back to Newtons physical laws-Whenever there is a move in the direction of anything or an "action" as Newton would put it, there is always a counter-action. This counter-action is simply something the average sheep like person has no idea about, "an invisible factor," so they just kind of move along like little sheep going to the slaughter.

Let's look at the chart on the next page to get a visual on how the Federal Reserve is making you broke.

The chart which follows is the dollar index which measures the value of the U.S. dollar in relation to a basket of other currencies which include the Euro (EUR), Yen (JPY), Pound (GBP),Canadian dollar (CAD), Krona (SEK), and Franc (CHF).

Just to demonstrate what is continuing to happen to the value of the dollar since we were forced off the gold standard, I placed the chart on the previous page for your viewing pleasure. Lets all send a letter of thanks to our congressmen.

The Fed's money printing policy is also punishing savers. Up until recently having a savings account or other investment vehicle that pays interest was a viable way to make your money grow. Today with Ben keeping interests rates at historic and unnatural lows, these investments have negative returns, that is, the interest rates being paid are below the rate of inflation.

The value of money.

If you were to go on safari and just happened to come across a tribe of natives and say you ran out of supplies, how would you go about getting them from the tribal leaders? I suppose you could whip out your wallet and try to exchange your greenbacks for what you needed, however it would not get you anything. Unless of course the tribe needed some paper to keep a fire going I suppose, otherwise the value of your money would be zero.

The value of money is an illusion.

Today money has no real value as demonstrated in the scenario above. Today we have a fiat money system. Fiat is a Latin term for "so let it be."

Here is how it works. The Federal Reserve which is not a part of the government and is in fact run by private banks and other individual's prints money out of thin air, **the same is if you were to make some counterfeit money at home using your computer and printer,** there is absolutely no difference. (Please do not do this, the Fed is allowed to, you are not).

This new money is then distributed to the central banks of the individual states which then liquefy, meaning they then lend that new money printed out of thin air to the commercial banks, and begin to charge interest on this money created from nothing.

So the Federal Reserve creates debt, which is all they create. The Fed prints money from nothing, literally out of thin air, and then that money "becomes real." This new money is then owed back to the Federal Reserve in the form of debt plus any interest it may accrue.

Wow, it must be great to be a central banker. Think about that scenario for a moment, the Federal Reserve creates debt owed to them plus interest from nothing. In my opinion this game played by the Fed is the most notorious scam in the history of the world, and I have more to say about this gag later on.

Before going off the gold standard the Federal Reserve was not able do this, that is it could not literally and simply just print money out of thin air, *money was real*, and that is the sole reason why money was so much more valuable at that time, up until 1971.

Each dollar printed by the Federal Reserve during the gold standard had to be backed, by law as stated in the U.S. Constitution, by an equal amount of precious metal, and each coin minted also had to have a percentage of precious metal in it, namely silver.

During the gold standard money represented the currency, *gold and silver,* which was backing and subsequently stored in government stockpiles. Each and every penny, nickel, dime, quarter, etc. as well as every subsequent bill represented that actual currency.

Today the money in your wallet, bank account, etc. has absolutely no intrinsic or real value.

The Federal Reserve bank prints money from nothing, literally out of thin air, and creates debt in the form of these said monies which is owed back to them plus any accrued interest.
And there my friend is the biggest scam which has ever been played upon the human race. But it gets much worse than that, read on.

Consider this for a moment. If you were to go on eBay right now and look at say a 1964 dime, it would probably bid up to about $3.25, that's because a 1964 dime actually had value because it contains a small amount of real silver. Gold and silver have been methods of exchange for thousands of years, in fact they are real currency and not money. During the gold standard money represented currency which is gold and silver, and as such you could have taken your money to any central bank and exchange that money for currency (gold and or silver) in the amount represented by that said money. Let's go back to the 1964 dime for a moment. So a 1964 dime is worth about $3.25 in today's money, what that means if we were still on a gold standard a gallon of gasoline would cost you just about a dime! Wow.

Going off the gold standard, under Nixon, did not come without a hefty price. What we have seen since going off the gold standard is an over 90% drop in the value of money. What this has done is crush the consumer or holder of money by destroying his purchasing power however, this rig has enriched the central bankers beyond anyone's imagination. Again they create debt owed to them plus interest from nothing. This is true for not just the Federal Reserve but all the worlds' central banks, which are also owned by the same people.

WARNING.
You had better sit down before reading this next segment. Please do.

If having a gold standard was so good, why was it abandoned in favor of a fiat money system?

To finance the Vietnam War, that is the answer. The U.S. government policymakers and the Military Industrial Complex needed to fund the Vietnam War, and with a gold standard in place they could not just print money out of thin air like they can and do today. So the central bankers came up with the brilliant idea, (brilliant for them), to abandon the gold standard and move to a fiat money system.

This way the government could have all the money they want, *as now with a fiat money system the Fed can simply print money out of thin air,* which made the Military Industrial Complex very happy, and in turn made the central bankers immensely wealthy. It was a win, win situation for those involved in running the war, but a horrible despicable loss for those who were forced spill their blood and guts on the battle fields of Vietnam via the draft, and humanity as a whole.

Why did we fight, and subsequently lose the Vietnam War anyway? O yes, to stop the spread of Communism.

69.

And how did the United States become involved in direct combat with the Vietcong?

Well we the American sheep, I mean people, were told that the Vietcong attacked one of our warships, a destroyer called the USS Maddox in what was known as the Gulf of Tonkin incident, 1964.

Now that is interesting, why would the Vietcong want to involve the United States in direct conflict? Why would they want to provoke the United States? In 1964 the Vietcong "navy" at that time consisted of antiquated WWII torpedo boats which were procured from France in the mid fifties.

Lets set the scene here for a moment. So you are a Vietcong General already heavily involved in armed conflict with the South Vietnamese government. At a critical juncture like that, would you consider or even attempt to attack a modern American warship? And if you did go ahead for some twisted reason decide to send your men directly to their deaths and attack this modern ship of war, a U.S. Destroyer, would you use antiquated torpedo boats?

Knowing that if you did the war could escalate and directly involve the United States? I don't think you would. The American people were told that on August 2nd 1964 the Vietcong attacked the U.S.S. Maddox with 3, left over from WWII, French torpedo boats therefore America had to enter into direct military conflict with the Vietcong. There are some who contend that the Gulf of Tonkin incident never even happened, and believe it was a story conjured up by the MIC to create a reason for the United States to get directly involved with the war. What ever the case may be, 58,209 American servicemen were killed. And we lost our gold standard.

WARNING IS STILL IN EFFECT.
This brings me to the next and third major player in this economic super game.
In section one I wrote about the politicocorporatists, that is the merger of the policymakers and the corporations and I also told you there was another major player involved. I am going to name them now, and I alluded to them in the previous pages. They are called the Military Industrial Complex.

Who or what is the Military Industrial Complex? The Military industrial complex abbreviated (MIC) is also called the Military industrial congressional complex and refers to the policies and monetary relationships between policymakers, the armed forces, and the corporations which supports them. These relationships include political contributions, congressional approval for defense spending, and other legislation which serves to further the interests of the MIC. Former President Eisenhower who before becoming President was a five star U.S. Army General during WWII filmed a warning to the American people about the MIC, I urge you to find it online and watch it.

So we lose our gold standard. **The Constitution of the United States Article I: No State shall coin Money; emit Bills of Credit; make anything but gold and silver Coin a Tender in Payment of Debt.** Does that sound like the creating of fiat money out of thin air to you?

But is gets better than that! And truly the simplicity of it is pure wicked brilliance on the part of the policymakers, the central banks, major corporations especially those involved in creating weapons and other war sustaining goods and lastly the MIC.

As we are aware, the sole reason why we were taken off a gold standard by our policymakers in direct and dastardly collusion with the central bankers was to finance the Vietnam War, there is no question about that. We are also aware that at the same time we were taken off our gold standard, the petrodollar system was instituted in an arrangement between the central bankers, the MIC, and OPEC, (organization of petroleum exporting countries). This arrangement created a system in which an ever increasing demand for the Federal Reserves fiat money would exist and the dollar would then become the worlds reserve currency.

It should be obvious to you at this point that the United States involvement in the Vietnam War was used as a ploy in what in my opinion was the most wretched scheme ever devised, this strategy succeeded in vaulting the Federal Reserves fiat money system into a method of enslavement of the world by debt owed to directly to the Federal Reserve/central banks.

I will also say: **this scheme although devious beyond any words I could possibly choose to put down on paper, may have been the most brilliant folly played upon the human race.**

Section 3.
Fear and Greed.

Market forces are only in part driven by supply and demand. Was it supply and demand which drove the cost of real estate to unrealistic levels? Absolutely not. How about if someone buys shares of stock in a company whose price to earnings, (PE) ratio, is 125:1? No to this one as well. So what does this tell us? Clearly supply and demand are not the only factors which drive the price of an item. The main driver of an asset is obviously not based upon fundamentals or a technical chart, it is psychological based upon perception.

As real estate prices began to soar into the stratosphere going way beyond what incomes and economic fundamentals would dictate, very few people were able to appreciate that there was a major problem developing. All kinds of excuses were made as to why real estate prices were going literally through the roof. But the root cause was greed and everyone wanted a piece of the cheesecake.

People see a particular asset rising fast, and as we all know people are always looking for that quick way to make money, so what happens is greed begins to pervade and overtake rational thinking and like a tidal wave, a frenzy of asset accumulation begins.

The problem with this behavior is frankly the general public lacks the knowledge needed to actually make these things work, so what happens is they end up get crushed, losing hefty sums on poor investments. The main reason for this is that way too many people tend to enter into a rising assets price at the high end, when the asset has already risen above realistic levels. Then people continue to hold onto this now toxic asset as the price corrects downward, leading to devastating losses.

This scenario is exactly what happened to multitudes of people who bought real estate at the top of the housing bubble, hoping to cash in.

Even at this point in time with the Federal Reserve holding tens of billions in toxic real estate assets, oh yes you remember, the ones they bought from the banks in order to bail them out because they made bad bets on these loans using U.S. Tax payer money? That wisdom along with the massive back log in foreclosed homes being held by these said banks, regardless of what action the Fed is taking to try and support housing prices at this level, real estate prices still have much further to fall. Which brings me to this: we humans have extremely short memories. The moral here is: at this point in time stay away from real estate, it's an awful time to buy a house as an investment despite what the main stream media is telling you. I will elaborate more on this during the last section of this book.

One more thing before I move on. If you are waiting for the value of your home to appreciate back up to or even near the top of the bubble, forget about it! Perhaps if you were to live 300 more years maybe, but not in yours or your children's lifetime. I am sorry to have to say this, but if you purchased your home at or near the top of the bubble you are now in possession of a toxic asset, and my advice to you is get out of it anyway you can.

Housing at a minimum, even from the point we are at today on a national level has to correct at least another 20 to 25% before it reaches fair market value.

Dot-Com.

From the mid 1990's up until the year 2002 we experienced the information technology boom and bust, also known as the dot-com bubble.
Take a look at this chart.

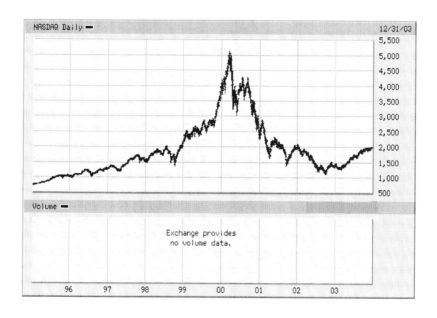

As you can see, the common theme in all these bubble charts is a meteoric rise followed by a crash or correction. Enormous amounts of money were both made and lost in each of these occurrences.

79.

The smart money is made on both sides of the bubbles, long positions on the rise and short positions on the fall. The problem with any asset bubble is not that they form, it's that people generally get in way to late, somewhere near the top and then tend to stay long the positions on the way down. The reasons for this type of behavior is lack of knowledge of how the game is played.

Now take a look at this chart.

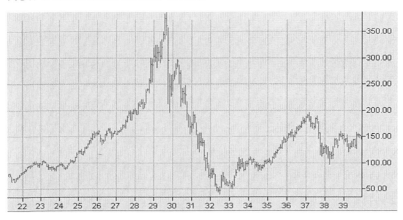

The chart above, *yes another clear bubble pattern*, is the stock market crash of 1929.

80.

So what caused the crash of 29'?

From 1925 to the third quarter of 1929 common stocks increased in value by 120 percent, that's it, period the end. There is no reason to open the history books and read possibly hundreds of pages or even perhaps several volumes of information on why the stock market crashed in 1929. For an asset, or any asset class for that matter to rise such a degree so fast is simply not sustainable or realistic.

So it all comes down to this, consumer sentiment, **the perception that the party would never end.**

Does any of this sound familiar to you? Its always the same story. Fundamentals, technical analysis, or any other measurable economic tool played no role.
How could the value of any asset rise outside that which average incomes may be and the rate of economic growth to such a degree? It does not make sense, and as such a bubble was formed and it subsequently popped period the end. I put this chart here for another reason.

I want to convey to you that these bubbles are in the grand scheme of things common occurrences and we are in the midst of the biggest bubble in human history right now.

In any asset bubble the up side is caused by greed, and on the down side of the bubble you have fear. I want you to notice the over-correction in this particular chart, I circled it on this next chart.

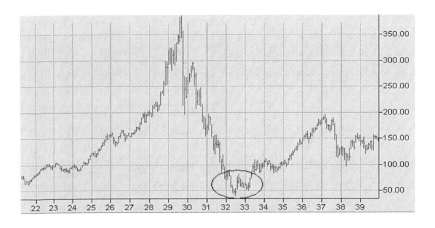

The reason a dropping asset tends to over-correct is because fear is actually stronger that greed.

This is why it is so important to understand human behavior.

Before I let the cat out of the bag, I will say this: the mother of all the bubbles ever created by man is already here, can you figure out what it is?

The next super bubble.

I mentioned that there was another bubble a few times already and I am going to elaborate on it at length in section 5. Taking advantage of this super bubble is why I wrote this book.

**I will tell you a secret, another super bubble is now in its very early stages right now, and that is something else we are going to capitalize on!

So I hope that I have established for you that greed brought on by a misguided perception is the single predominant factor in why all these asset bubbles were created, and it is also what we insiders count on. Insiders, like you are becoming now, simply sit and wait while all the sheep, *the uninformed fly by the seat of their pants type of people,* line up for the slaughter and then they give it to them good.

Its not that these sheep like people types deserve it, they just either do not have the foresight, lack sufficient drive, cannot think outside the box, and a host of other things.

My point is I wish more people would at least try to understand those things which have enormous potential to both help and hurt them and their families.

I wish people would read more, educate themselves, but unfortunately most will not.
In any game there are winners and there are losers and that's the way it is. It is like poker, which is a game I play a lot of. We sit and lurk like hungry sharks just waiting for the "donkeys" as we call them to sit down at the table with us, and then we eat their lunch for them and we leave the table with their money. Why do these donkeys lose their money? We are not any smarter than they are, we just understand how the game is played to a higher degree because we study it.

We are willing to put the required time in to learn the game.

Let me say this, if you have gotten through the information I have presented thus far in this book and are beginning to grasp some of these concepts you are way ahead of the game already, and I am personally proud of you. There is a huge amount of information here.

Not only is it greed which drives the price of an asset way beyond with the fundamentals dictate, it is also greed that causes these same people to lose ridiculous amounts of money. These people, just like the donks at the poker table are entering into a realm they should never have gotten into in the first place and why? Because their greed, or visions of grandeur get the better of them.

Fear.
We have discussed in earlier sections of this book how fear is used as a tool to influence human behavior. It is also fear which is a driver of an assets price, in this case downward pressure.

What tends to happen when an asset price or the overall market falls rapidly it tends to over-correct That is the price falls below its fair market value and this is when a real buying opportunity occurs.

Earlier on in section 1, I presented you with a chart of the U.S. housing price index. What I suspect would have happened if the Fed had not stepped in and tried to pump the housing prices back up, (something that has no chance of working in the long run because the massive and powerful market forces will eventually prevail for reasons I discuss throughout this book), is housing would have continued to drop to the point of over-correction. This scenario is still going to occur and I will discuss more on this in section 4 .

More greed.

As outlined in the previous section, under President Nixon and the MIC along with the central banks we lost our gold standard. This move although brilliant for some ensuring massive financial wealth and a virtual endless supply of "fake"money to fight the Vietnam War as well as

any other war the MIC wishes to force upon the American people, dealt a devastating blow to the common people. As the value of the now fiat dollar began its long and precipitous dive sucking the purchasing power away from the consumer, the petrodollar system was created.
Now with this new petrodollar system the worlds consumers could now be enslaved by the U.S. central banks virtually worthless printed money.
Just to get another visual on how going from a gold standard to a fiat system has affected the value of the dollar, I am going to put a chart here again on the next page to remind you.

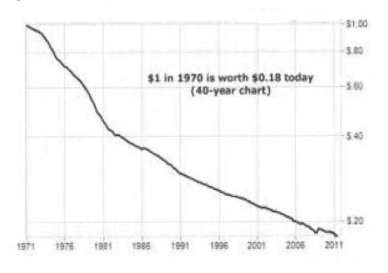

87.

What the petrodollar system succeeded in doing is guarantee that the world would now have an essential need for the U.S. central banks fiat money. Here is how it works. In return for U.S. military protection of their oil, the OPEC cartel would agree to price their oil in U.S. dollars. What this means is that any nation wishing to acquire oil from OPEC would have to exchange their money for U.S. fiat money in order to purchase OPEC oil. Now with this petrodollar system a massive, sustained, and ever increasing global demand for the Feds fiat money was created, and subsequently because of this the dollar becomes the worlds reserve currency.

Admittedly this was true brilliance in action for the worlds central bankers. They now can create unimaginable wealth by issuing debt to the world, now this is greed in the extreme.

So, here we have the most powerful military the world has ever known protecting OPEC nations oil. OPEC nations include Iraq, Kuwait, Libya, Saudi Arabia, United Arab Emirates, Qatar, Iran, Nigeria, Algeria, Angola, Ecuador, and Venezuela (12 nations).

88.

Let's look at this a bit more closely. We already have Iraq, Kuwait, and Libya under direct U.S. military control, that's 25% so far and there will be others in the near future. You would have to be blind to not see what is going on here. It is not enough that these countries had agreed to price their oil in the Feds fiat money, they, the politicocorporatists along with the MIC want control of the physical oil.

I suppose the real question is this, why do they want control of the physical oil? Lets look at another chart.

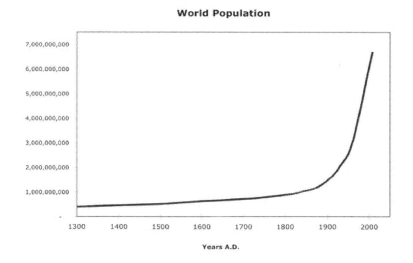

World Population

The chart above demonstrates the world population boom which we are currently in, *this particular chart is a bit behind the times actually as we have just crossed the seven billion mark.*
However, what is important to be aware of here is it appears we are in a massive population bubble. The truth is yes, the exponential rise in the population is causing great strain on the worlds natural resources.

Which brings us back to why the politicocorporatists and the MIC want control of the physical oil. But before I elaborate on peak oil, I want you to look at another chart.

This next chart demonstrates what has happened/is happening to the price of corn from March 2010 to April 2011. In one years time it has doubled in price. We all shop for food, so I do not have to tell you what is happening to the price of food items however, I will tell you that that these prices are going to get much higher. It is clear that commodities such as corn are going to be in an ever increasing demand as the world population continues to grow. The same is true for oil.

The life blood of the Earth is oil.

No single other item has influenced the world more than oil. Oil in many ways has taken us from the dark ages into our modern world. On average one 42 gallon barrel of oil creates 19.5 gallons of gasoline, and the rest is used to make other items. In fact thousands of common items are made from petrochemicals.

That brings us to this, peak oil.

Is the world running out of oil? Probably not at this time. Perhaps someday there will be no oil left, however this may not occur for a very long time, how long? Who knows. Understand, I am not trying to make little of the situation and I do realize clearly that alternative sources of energy need to be explored. With that, the problem is not how much oil may or may not be left, its about how much is available and how quickly in can be pulled from the ground. That is the situation we are in right now.

The demand for oil is frankly enormous, beyond enormous actually and growing every day. And at this time there is no clear solutions to keep up with this demand.

Earlier I presented you with a chart showing the booming global population, much of that is from Asia. The demand for energy from Asia has now taken over the demand from the western world. The United States was the prime consumer of energy in the world, now it is Asia.

The population boom is now in a positive feedback loop, growing populations begets an ever growing population exponentially.

The swelling population of the Earth is in part due to people living longer because the the advancement of medicine, nutrition, among other things as well. But world population is also increasing because the birth survival rates are now much higher in the underdeveloped parts of the world.

This positive feedback population boom is in a bubble, and at one point there will be a correction. Again it is the same situation, you have a population expanding at a rate far above what incomes, human resources, or global Gross Domestic Product dictates, therefore as in every other bubble it becomes and is not sustainable by any means. We are already witnessing what strained natural resources are doing to the unfortunate peoples of third world countries, disease, starvation, and overall human suffering are at all time historic highs.

And let me say this, as a provider of health care this is something that hits home for me.

Commodities are prophetic.

Take a look at this chart.

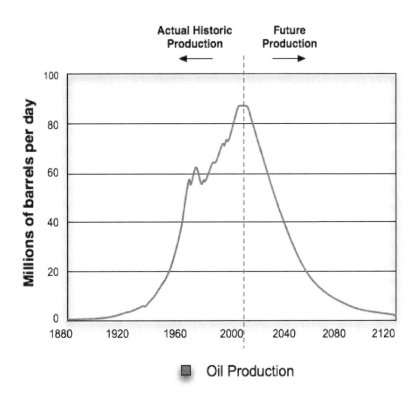

Can you say bubble?

Look at the run up in the production of oil from the 1920's until today.

Peak oil is a term which is commonly used to define that point in time when the maximum rate of global oil extraction and therefore production is reached, after that time the rate of production enters terminal decline.

A strong case can be made that we are in that period of time now. As we know, the demand for oil is continuing to grow and has no chance of slowing until an alternative energy source is either discovered or created.

The massive population boom/bubble at this time guarantees a massive and ever growing demand for oil. However is appears that with all the resources available to us at this time the extraction and therefore production of oil has peaked. From the 1930's up until the 1970's the extraction and production of oil rose steadily. Since that time the production of oil based upon demand has slowed dramatically, and without an alternative source of energy the gap between the production of oil verses demand is going to continue to widen.

This strain on natural resources is going on across the board, earlier I presented you with a chart demonstrating what is happening with the price of corn. I chose corn because thousands of commonly used items contain corn and the demand for more of it is only going to rise. The prices of all commodities have no where to go but up because of the population bubble, as well as the continued attack on the value of the dollar by the Federal Reserve as these items are priced in U.S. Dollars..

More fear.

As of late all we hear about by the main stream media is the threat Iran potentially poses by acquiring nuclear weapons. The politicocorporatists and the MIC it seems have chosen their next target, yet another OPEC nation, and they are playing the fear card on not only the American common people but also the world's. They played the same card with the run up and subsequent Iraq war/takeover. Remember the whole weapons of mass destruction lie? The repeated showing of atomic explosions by the mainstream media?

How about how every member of the Bush administration would utter the words "mushroom cloud" whenever they had the chance on national television. How about how we were told of the undeniable proof regarding the existence of these weapons of mass destruction by British Prime Minister Tony Blair? I could go on and on but lets move to this: they recently got to take Libya by playing yet another set of cards.

The first card they played was rehashing the Lockerbie bomber's warm welcome when he returned to Libya causing people to get angry and wanting revenge. This "playing on the psyche" of the masses was being set up long before the actual "kinetic military action" as it was called. O yes, it was not a war because there was no American boots on the ground, another untruth by the way.

American intelligence was on the ground months prior to the bombs being dropped and how do I know that? I was a military officer and I know how the system works, I am also very familiar with military tactics.

The next folly card which was played by the MIC was this: "*we have to drop an enormous amount of munitions on the Libyan government "for humanitarian reasons," because Qaddafi is turning his military on his own people.* Keep in mind that in Syria at this time the situation is much worse, the Syrian government right now as you are reading this is virtually exterminating the general public/any opposition to the status-quo. Also keep in mind that Syria is not a member of OPEC, if they were, American bombers would now be in the skies over Syria, they would have to be. As you know the petrodollar accord states: **the United States military must protect the oil of OPEC nations in order to preserve the U.S. dollar as the worlds reserve currency.**

The Libyan takeover.

First they set up the "action" by creating global public anger at the Libyan government over the Lockerbie bomber, then they use the civil war in Libya as an excuse to go in and establish a military presence to take control of the physical oil. Very simple and straightforward.

Another reason Iran now has a target painted over it is this: Iran is the only OPEC nation which will sell its oil to another nation, namely Russia, not based in U.S. Dollars thus violating their petrodollar agreement.

I am not sure if the main stream media is a party to all this manipulation or they are just literal talking heads being force fed whatever information they convey to the public. In any case there is very little real journalism anymore. There are some in the main stream media who I do respect greatly, for example Rick Santelli, and there are a few others. I often wonder how or even why some of those in the media got there in the first place? It is obvious that they have very limited insight about the issues which they "report on." As the day progresses, sometimes on a minute to minute basis their story changes with the DOW, it is actually funny to watch.

With regard to the DOW, do you realize it has been basically flat since the year 2000? In the year 2000 we hit DOW 11,500 and today here at the end of 2011 it is, well actually a bit less that that. So all this talk of rally's, this or that with regard to the DOW is just fluff in an attempt to affect perception.

Now if you priced the DOW against gold, the DOW has gotten slaughtered-but no one is reporting on that!

.

Section 4.
A financial wrecking ball is headed our way.

The central banks, the politicocorporatists, and the Wall Street insiders are all keenly aware of the fact that the financial end game is at hand. However, they don't really care and why is that? That is because all of them know how to "play the game." They are fully conscious of how this gamy will conclude and therefore they are positioning themselves accordingly. Your turn is coming soon.

My mission with the undertaking of this book project is to try my best and demonstrate to you as clearly as possible how important it is to know the parameters of this game, and I hope I have done that thus far. Now that you have an understanding of some of both the invisible and ominous factors involved in their **politicocorporatisticmilitarianism dogma,** *(a term I conjured up which encompasses the three major players in this economic mega game and their agenda),* and how it is more or less designed to keep the vast majority of people in a sheep like state,

lets go back and look at a few charts and concepts.
I have laid out these next few pages in kind of a time line
manner for you.

Housing bubble chart.

As we know, at this time the Fed is in desperation mode
made clear through the 300% increase in the monetary
base in a futile attempt to stop the falling real estate
market. The Fed has also succeeded as well in bailing
out the banks by purchasing tens of billions of toxic
assets with tax payer money.

The Fed is also subsequently, by printing more money out of thin air, purchased/is purchasing long term treasury bonds in order to keep interest rates below fair market value. What the Fed has done thus far is slow the drop in real estate by not allowing natural market dynamics to decide fair market value. In other words what Ben has succeeded in doing is not allowed a natural correction to occur at this point. Mr. Bernanke has also been successful in creating an ever swelling and gargantuan dollar bubble, the largest the world has ever known, and this can be visualized in this next chart.

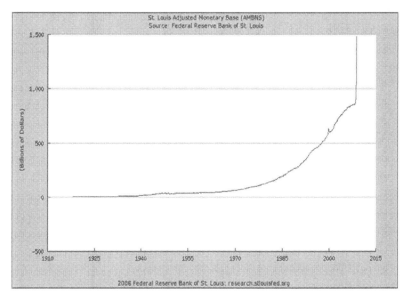

This dollar bubble given to us again by the illustrious Ben Bernanke, has done this to the value of the dollar in one year. Take a look at the chart below.

Now as we know, in order for Ben to keep this all going he has had to print money out of thin air and purchase treasury bonds in order to keep interest rates artificially low, purchasing these bonds also helps finance the day to day operations of the United States.

This has caused yet another bubble to develop, and this bubble is THE MOTHER OF THEM ALL. It is the U.S. DEBT BUBBLE.

Here is what it looks like, next page. (This chart does take the liberty of projecting what the debt will be in a year or two).

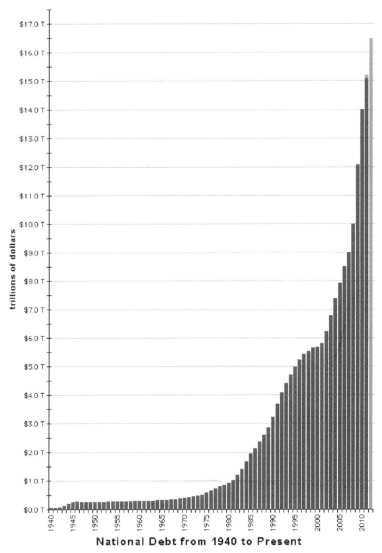

National Debt from 1940 to Present

Source: U.S. National Debt Clock
http://www.brillig.com/debt_clock/

106.

Today the headlines read: "Stocks succumb to Europe," and "European Debt Crushed U.S. Markets," etc, etc. Never once do they mention that not only is the United States the biggest debtor nation in the history of the world with debt problems which eclipse that of Europe by exponents, problems which it will be facing in the near future. They, and you know who they are by now, are trying as hard as they can to cause it to seem like the United States is isolated from these problems and nothing could possibly be farther from the truth.

Well there it is, the mother of all bubbles.

Just about a week ago the U.S. debt ballooned to over 15,000,000,000.00, (fifteen trillion dollars), and now represents more than 100% of Gross Domestic Product (GDP). Interestingly, even though this is a grim historic event for the United States it has gotten almost no media coverage, why do you think that is? Simple, it would affect consumer sentiment in a negative way.

I believe a better way to think about the national debt is this: at this point in time the national debt is greater than seven times, actually closer to eight times, the total amount of tax revenue collected from the American people in a year and growing faster every day. The national debt is growing by about twenty five thousand dollars a second and this number will accelerate as the debt and subsequent interest accrue.

Now lets say you are a lender, would you give a loan to any entity who's debt to income ratio was nearing 8 to 1 and growing with no end in sight? Not only is there no end in sight, the projections of where this galactic number will be going just over the next few years is staggering. In other words there is absolutely no possible way for the debt to be repaid, and as soon as people get hip to that with a roar like thunder it is all coming down.

Each week the government holds auctions for its treasury bonds, these bonds as you are aware finance everything that is needed to keep America running.

In Europe as of late the auctions for their bonds are not going so well, and because of that the yields on their bonds are moving higher and higher. The reason for that is as these bonds are perceived as riskier investments and in order for someone to buy them they expect a greater return on their money, very simple. Now, here in the U.S. bond yields are at record lows for some of the reasons we have been covering, like the Federal Reserve buying them with printed out of thin air money. The other reason is people still have their blinders on, therefore they continue to invest in long term U.S. bonds even though the interest earned by them is lower than the expected rate of inflation! That should explain to you how desperate the situation in Europe really is despite what you here in the main stream media.

Lets talk a little more about the U.S. Debt.
Think about this a bit more for a moment, at just this point the tax revenue collected from the American people does not even cover the day to day expenses of running the country, it covers about 60% of them, the other 40%

continues to be borrowed and this ratio is going to get much worse.

Now again you are a loan officer, would you even remotely consider granting a loan to this client?
I am sorry sir, but it seems you have run out of credit. Have a nice day.

Uncle Sam's pockets have been picked dry, and he has run up truly epic amounts of debt. Our country is completely broke and has to rely on other country's, investors, and the Federal Reserve as a lender of last resort to keep it propped up and running. I love this country, and as I sit here writing this trying desperately to warn as many people as I can of her impending collapse I honestly have to hold back tears. What a shame, what have we done? Are we all not a party to this action?

Collapse by design?

There are those who believe that America is being caused to collapse deliberately, being brought forth by clandestine groups like the Illuminati for example. These individuals site certain symbols like these, (see image below), which can be found on any dollar bill however, I do not agree that by design America is being caused to collapse.

Some say it is the Free Masons whom are helping to destroy America. Freemasonry is an order which many of our founding fathers were a member to and still thrives today.

I believe it is generally easier for people to believe that some kind of grand, bordering on the supernatural scheme is responsible for the crisis we are in and subsequent ruination we are going to face, then to accept that natural forces combined with ineptitude, greed, and corruption are really to blame. The fall of the Soviet Union was brought about by the same triad, ineptitude, greed, and corruption.

In a strange twist this is also true: *the bigger the lie the easier it is for people to believe it.*

The wrecking ball cometh.

The U.S. Debt bubble can also be called the dollar bubble, which is likewise the bond bubble. All of these are three parts of the same thing, and each is squarely dependent and an integral part of the other.

The deficit which is the national debt is borrowed dollars, so here you have the connection between the debt bubble and the dollar bubble. The bond market represents IOU's, (to be paid with interest of course), which are also priced in dollars and added to the national debt, therefore as you can see each of these are a part of the same enormous three part mega bubble.
And both you and I know what happens to economic bubbles.

All economic bubbles without exception have to pop because they rise beyond levels which are able to be sustained by any means. *So as I have been saying throughout this book, whatever scheme the U.S. Government, the Federal Reserve , the European Central Bank (ECB), the International Monetary Fund (IMF), the European Union (EU), or any governments act, or program attempts to do will fail over time, it is a mathematical certainty.*
I will repeat this again, all economic bubbles cannot be sustained by ANY means.

All that can be done is defer the inevitable, and this postponement is the worst possible thing that can be done. All putting off or propping up the massive already hyper-inflated bubbles does is achieve in creating bigger, much more dangerous and devastating apocalyptic monster debt bubbles.

These bubbles, the debt, dollar, and bond bubbles are going to pop, and there is no question about it. Any argument to the contrary is simply utter nonsense as theses mega bubbles cannot be sustained by any means.

Now if the policymakers had the guts to make extreme cuts across the board beginning with slashing almost to non existence the entitlement programs, every piece of government pork, and stop policing the world while at the same time cutting taxes for the American people well then they can solve the problem.

However that scenario has absolutely no chance of happening for several reasons most of which almost need no explanation, but the one reason which does warrant explanation and is not blatantly obvious is this: **the concept of greed to the extreme.**

Please allow me to explain. I began this book project with the hope that I would be able to covey a message in such a way that it would allow people to have a better understanding of how this game is played. That I could just lay this all out in plain, clear, language which would enable anyone, not just someone with a PhD or a five hundred thousand dollar portfolio to grasp the folly which is being played on not just the American people, but the peoples of the world.

The greatest threat to humankind.

With that said: the policymakers, corporate insiders, and the Military Industrial Complex have twisted and allowed to happen the creation of the most monstrous threat to the peoples of the world, the three pronged unsustainable debt bubbles which include the national deficit, the dollar, and the bond market.

This global debt issue must be understood for what is really is, if you were to weigh out the dangers posed against the peoples of the world with respect to what has the potential to affect more lives and cause more devastation across the board which would include famine and death, the elephantine global debt bubble is equally on par with a global nuclear exchange.

Is it insanity or brilliance?
I suppose that depends of which side of the equation you are on, there are always two sides, but allow me to put a perspective on this. I am not a religious guy, but let's call the policymakers, corporate insiders, and the MIC collectively the "diabolical trinity," and this trinity has an agenda.

On several occasions in this book I have eluded to the fact that the three main players in this game are positioning themselves for the fateful crash, for which you are now aware involves the three pronged mega bubbles bursting. What we are going to be doing is placing ourselves in much the same position as they, which is the opposite side of the equation unfortunately for the general uninformed public. Understand, there is no "lack of will" by the policymakers to change these things, which is something we hear quite often in the main stream media, these people along with the other two participants which encompass this diabolical trinity at this point are being motivated by the end game, and greed is the main driver here.

The diabolical trinity is well aware of this three pronged super bubble, and they are actually counting on its bursting sometime in the near future. In fact the bursting of these bubbles is the main facilitator of why they want to and are continuing to inflate it, and that is because the bigger they can make this bubble the more wealth they can create for themselves when it ultimately pops.

It basically comes down to a simple transaction, in fact the largest transfer of wealth the world has ever seen is already well underway and will begin to move with ever increasing speed as the three pronged debt bubble begins its downward trajectory.

117.

Of course the other side of the equation is this: that wealth they are banking on has to come from somewhere, and it is going to be driven by fear to the extreme as the general population goes scrambling to sell all of their assets as their value plummets. Assets like real estate, 401K's, pension plans, equities, government bonds, are all going to suffer terrible and sustained losses because at this point they will have become toxic assets which is defined as *"assets whose value has fallen significantly and for which there is no longer a functioning market, so that such assets cannot be sold at a price satisfactory to the holder."*
What will then follow as the people who did not see this coming or chose not to heed warnings from people like myself and others will now have lost their faith **by force.**

This will lead to mass "bank runs," and a vast majority of those seeking to withdraw their funds will get nothing, and the FDIC (Federal Deposit Insurance Corporation) will not be able to help either as they too will be affected and have to declare bankruptcy, *within the confines of the situation presented.*

118.

And the (paper) wealth of the vast majority of the population of the United States and the world, will be completely wiped out with no way for it to be recovered.

Most people do not realize that the money which "exists" in their accounts is actually not there, it exists as digital numbers only. All banks in order to make a profit have to lend out the money they take in as deposits, and that money is lent out on a multiplier. Here is how it works: You deposit $500.00 into one of your accounts, the bank is then allowed to multiply this deposit by a factor of ten and now is able to loan out $4,500.00. All banks and credit unions operate in this manner. A bank is only required to keep a fraction of its customers deposits on site, so in the event of a "bank run" as you can see, just a fraction of the depositors is going to get their money. As for the rest, destitution which will lead to desperation.

This brings us back to the agenda of the fore aptly named diabolical trinity. Here is their agenda: as I stated earlier the wealth which will be lost by the general public is going to be "up for grabs" and collected by those who understand the rules, and can play the game.

As the three pronged bubble bursts and public assets become toxic panic will ensue and fear will create a mass wave of selling, and no one wants to be the last one out the door because there will be a point when there will be no buyers for these toxic assets.

At this point even the Fed will not be able to come to the rescue because the dollar bubble will have already burst, and massive and uncontrolled inflation will already be upon us.

As aggregate public panic selling driven by fear continues, and the value of most assets across the board are plummeting, a massive transfer of wealth is going to be taking place. **And the use of "mass" in this case is an grave understatement.**

Keep in mind, all this money created by the selling of these assets has to go somewhere and I will give you one guess who is going to be on the other side of this equation to collect it, yes, the diabolical trinity..**And you.**

Understand this does not make you a bad person, at this point it is just the smart thing to do as you now have understanding of how the end game is going to play out and you have every right to protect yourself and your family. I am going to detail in section 5 the necessary steps which you should be taking in order for you to capitalize of these sequences of events, but for now it is important to gain some more insight. Please keep in mind this is not personal, its business which we are talking about. You are not looking to screw anyone, it is about making the right decision based upon knowledge available to anyone, period.

What the Fed has effectively done is create a dollar/bond/debt bubble of truly nightmare proportions. It is far and away the biggest bubble ever created by man.

At this point in time with the European debt crisis in its early stages and what it appears as a successful campaign by the politicocorporatists in trying to keep the public eye off the ball, that is convincing the world that the United States is isolated from these debt issues, U.S. treasury bonds have been selling. In fact the rally in the bond market for someone like me who actually understands what is going on is baffling.

However, I believe that it is fear which is the main driver here and fear causes rational people to do irrational things. Understand, these U.S. bonds are paying negative returns and are still being purchased at an ever increasing rate! That should give you an idea of how desperate and fearful people are regarding the European debt problem.

Let's lay it all out on the table. What solutions do the European politicocorporatists have? They have only two. The first is to allow natural market forces to intervene which would cause immediate and massive asset losses across the board, or the second option:

have the central banks fire up the printing presses and stave off the inevitable collapse for a few more years. Which one do you think they are going to choose?

By choosing option number two like the Federal Reserve already has, they will be successful in accomplishing a temporarily pushing off a much bigger and devastating collapse. What the central banks of the world are going to do beyond a shadow of a doubt is push this thing off as much as possible, and how they will do that is by printing massive amounts of money out of thin air. The farther they can push this off, because that is all they can do, the worse the inevitable collapse of the three pronged debt mega bubble is going to be. For those on the other side of the equation there is this: the more mass that can put into the debt, the greater the pay off is going to be.

Understand in every game there are winners and there are losers, **it all boils down to a simple exchange.**

As this scenario plays out and we are seeing this happen now, there is going to be deflation, but this is just the initial phase.

This deflationary period has no choice but to turn into massive inflation within a very short time, and this is because all this money which the central banks are going to print is going to devalue the money globally and exponentially.

As we know the Federal Reserve has increased the monetary base 300% since 2008. However as of late we are not seeing any real inflation, yet. Part of the reason for this the Fed is requiring banks to keep monies in reserve, which is something that is never done because if the banks do not loan out money, they make no profit. What the Fed is doing in an attempt to control the flow of all this extra money is paying the banks interest on the monies it keeps in reserve. What the banks are doing is keeping extra money over and above their Fed requirement in their reserves, because the Fed is essentially paying them to do it.

At this time it is in the banks best interest to keep this extra money in their reserves being that the Fed is paying them interest on this money, but for the economy this does not come without a price. It is actually a double edge sword, on one side of the equation having this extra money in the banks reserves keeps it from making its way out into the consumer side of the money supply and causing inflation. But the other side of the equation is it keeps banks from lending, essentially freezing up consumer credit which keeps the economy from expanding. And of course the Fed is paying the interest to the banks for their increased reserves with more money printed out of thin air, and what does this do? It continues to increase the monetary base and thus puts even more downward pressure on the value of the dollar. The sluggish economy is also responsible for slowing the rate at which the Feds liquidity enters circulation, this phenomenon occurs simply because people are not spending money, or seeking loans. Therefore the extra "liquid," money, stays out of the consumer side of the monetary base.

At this point in time we are seeing the European bond yields rise and the U. S. bond yields drop. We are seeing this because the world still does not "get it" and realize that U.S. debt is not a safe haven.

Sure the U.S. can pay back any debt which includes the deficit in full at anytime, but it would have to do that by having Ben print it all out of thin air which would in turn reduce the dollar value to zero.

So it appears that Europe has just about maxed out their credit card, here in the U.S. fear is allowing us to still acquire credit and therefore more debt, and judging from the bond rally I suspect this will continue for a while. Today it seems people are losing interest in what they consider riskier assets namely the equity market. However, they are willing to purchase treasury bonds which offer negative returns. What I know is there is no way the Federal Reserve is going to allow the equity markets or the real estate markets to collapse before increasing the monetary base a thousand percent more than the three hundred percent they already have. With this Knowledge, equities are the place to be and not bonds which offer negative returns.

At some point the central banks are going to be "the lenders of last resort," and this will come about simply because those who were purchasing U.S. Debt will have finally woken up to the fact that the debt can never be paid back, and at this point the end game will be imminent. Once the bond auctions begin to fail, and in Europe currently these auctions are already getting weaker, either the central banks have to step in and buy or the party is over, again what do you think is the most likely scenario?

In either situation interest rates will have to rise and this will push the recession button even harder, people will cut back on spending, businesses will close, unemployment will rise, less tax revenue will be collected, the central banks will have to print more money, and the value of the money will continue to decline.

Because the central banks of the world will be printing money out of thin air for as long as they possibly can the astronomical three pronged debt bubble of the United States, and those in Europe will continue to inflate.

At the point when the debt/dollar/bond bubble of the United States begins to collapse, something which is a mathematical certainty, every remaining bubble left on Earth will also simultaneously pop as well.

Section 5.
There is a Silver Lining.

Having an understanding of how this game is going to play out gives us enormous opportunity.

History has shown us that it is in times of great economic distress those who understand just a few basic rules make fortunes, and perhaps more importantly have survived.

Being armed with an understanding of how the game works makes it easy for us to determine what actions by the governing bodies are going to be undertaken, and with this knowledge it is easy to make decisions.

With this evolving and fast moving global financial crisis moving ever closer, the time to place yourself into an adventitious position is now. The general public is woefully prepared for what is coming and that is because the American culture today virtually guarantees failure. Today far too many people are dependent on the government for their existence.

Entitlement programs in this country have created legions of what would have been viable people who contribute to society in a meaningful way into people who have learned not to take care of themselves, and that is what scares me the most.

It is simple to deduce that there is no real or meaningful economic recovery here in the United States, and the global economy is showing ever increasing signs of great financial instability. I unfortunately believe that among developed nations the American public is going to suffer the most as this crisis deepens because so many are dependent on government support.

The current situation is this: right now virtually anyone can put his or her self into a position in which a great deal of money will be made as this crisis develops. **In fact there has never been a better time in the history of the world where an individual with little or no net worth at this time can become wealthy.**

Let's talk.

I hope that I have already established that the one place that you do not want to be is in cash, *that is unless you are an individual with experience in shorting bonds.* We know that the central banks of the world are going to print enormous amounts of money to try and stave off the popping of the debt/dollar/bond bubbles as long as possible and this is going to punish the value of money to the point of ridiculousness.

We also know that as the three pronged bubble's inevitable fall accelerates, global bond yields are going to rise dramatically. The Fed has made it clear that they are going to keep interest rates at these artificial/historic lows until at least 2013, what happens then? The Fed cannot lower rates any more, as we already know the yields of long term treasuries is negative, so the only way interest rates have to go is up. At one point no matter how or what the Fed or other world central banks do it will be the market that dictates fair market value with regard to interest rates, and what we may see at that point is an uncontrolled, rapid rise in these rates due to uncontrollable fear which is going to pervade the bond market.

As treasury bonds sell off and interest rates rise, the equity markets too are going to sell off and I believe rapidly at this point. With the sell off in equities and T-bills, (Treasury Bonds), this extra cash is going to look for a place to go and that place is into commodities. At this point in the sequence the already rising commodity prices are going to spike across the board, and inflation is going to make it very difficult for people to obtain even basic necessities.

I am certain that the biggest spike in commodity prices is going to be in crude oil and precious metals.

Now if you are a savvy trader with a lot experience in these things, an excellent position for you to be in at this point in the sequence would be short positions almost across the board, but especially bonds and financial stocks.

If you are just the average Joe you should be taking up long positions in commodities, especially energy and mining companies. If you are even less savvy than the average Joe and only have a small, or almost no amount to invest no worries, I have a plan for you as well which I will elaborate on later.

Take a look the chart below. What this chart demonstrates is the DOW/Gold ratio over time, (since 1900). As you can see there are repeating phases here, that is there are times in which the price of one ounce of gold equals the DOW.

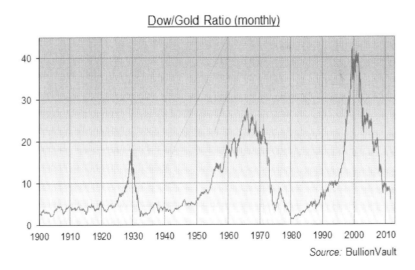

Dow/Gold Ratio (monthly)

Source: BullionVault

133.

Do you see a pattern here?

It appears that we are now nearing a position in this sequence where the Dow/Gold ratio is going to correct to one to one however, we are in no ordinary times right now and I believe we are going to correct better than the one to one ratios which this chart is historically demonstrating. An over-correction is going to take place.

At a minimum sometime in the near future this ratio will be at least one to one, but I believe almost beyond any doubt that fear and greed are going to push this ratio to better than the historic one to one.

The main driver here is going to be all these dollars fleeing the bond markets which will cause yields and interest rates to rise, which in turn will put downward pressure on the equity market. As the equity market along with the bonds fall the price of gold will rise until the historic one to one ratio is achieved however, we have never been in a situation like the current financial crisis. We are in the midst of a massive debt/dollar/bond bubble, and when this bubble pops the Fed will be almost powerless to stop it therefore again,

134.

I am expecting to see an over-correction.

Why I am saying the Fed will be "almost" powerless to stop it? Because there is one thing the Fed can do, and that one thing would me to peg the dollar to a hard asset like gold.

However by the time the Fed would even consider pegging the dollar to an asset like gold the price would have probably more that quadrupled from where is it today which is about $1,700.00 an ounce. In fact I am just about certain that gold in any situation is going to go much higher than quadruple today's price.

I will also say something else, I believe that as this situation plays out we are going to be seeing a dramatic discrepancy between the commodities exchange, (COMEX), spot price or "paper" gold and the bullion price, the same goes for silver.
What is going to drive the price differential between spot and bullion is this: fear. Fear is going to cause a massive, sustained, and increasing demand for gold,

and silver, and this demand is quickly going to overwhelm the supply which the COMEX claims it has. Once the COMEX becomes overwhelmed and cannot deliver on the orders being placed for physical delivery of the metals, bullion prices are going to rise exponentially.

***I am certain beyond any doubt that the next bubble which is going to be created is a gold super bubble, you can quote me on this and I believe I am the first to be publishing this prediction. Lets see if I am right!**

The popping of the three pronged debt bubble, (deficit/dollar/bond), is going to cause a major downward correction in every asset class across the board, (except commodities especially oil and precious metals), however fear is going to cause an over-correction.

.

The reason why I keep bringing up my theory of an over-correction is because at that point, and this expands upon my gold super bubble theory, we are going to want to get our money out of certain assets and into the distressed assets which are going to be created by the bursting of the three pronged mega bubble.

And this is how we are going to create our dynasty.

Don't buy gold.

As we know asset bubbles are a common part of history and when the debt/dollar/bond bubble deflates it is going to create yet another bubble, a super bubble I believe, and that bubble is going to be a gold super bubble. This next super bubble is going to create massive wealth for those who understand how this financial crisis is going to play out however I am not advocating that you invest in gold.

I am advising you to invest in silver instead.

Is there anything wrong with buying gold? Absolutely not, and if you do buy gold you will make huge profits but consider this. The silver to gold ratio currently is about 50 to 1, and historically this ratio is about 15 to 1, what this means is at this time silver is grossly undervalued and promises to outperform gold in terms of return on your investment. In the midst of the gold super bubble which I am predicting,

137.

the multiples created by holding silver are going to be staggering.

Take a look at the chart below.

This chart is again the DOW/gold ratio over time however, in this particular chart I have included trend lines at both the peaks and troughs. It is easy to get a visual on where is appears this is going. It also appears

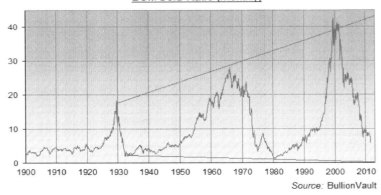

Dow/Gold Ratio (monthly)

Source: BullionVault

that this ratio will indeed be better than one to one favoring gold.

It is no secret that central banks of the world who for the past several decades have been net sellers of gold are now acquiring it in mass.

138.

In fact never before in history since the inception of central banking has their been a time in which the accumulation of gold by these institutions has been so great.

Question: do you think they know something which they do not want the general population to know?
Answer: without a doubt yes.

Fact: *if people simply instead of depositing their paychecks of the Federal Reserves fiat paper just took a percentage of that paper money and converted in into real currency like gold or silver, instead of becoming poorer each day the Fed prints more of their counterfeit money they would be getting richer. This also has another beneficial effect, each time someone exchanges their fake paper wealth for real wealth in the form of gold and silver they take power away from the central bankers.*

It is the easiest thing to do, and you would be creating real wealth for yourself while at the same taking it away from the central bankers. (And this should be your counter-action to the Fed's policy of devaluing the dollar.)

At the beginning of this segment I started off with "don't buy gold," I really did not mean you shouldn't buy gold. Buying gold, or to put it another way exchanging the Federal Reserves fiat paper money for real currency like gold is without a doubt one of the best things that you can do to create wealth in the coming years however it is not the best thing.

Accumulate as much silver as you can possibly get your hands on.

As you know I am predicting the next bubble right here and now, and that is going to be a gold super bubble driven by people having lost their faith in this fake, fiat, Ponzi scheme based economy. The loss in faith is going to be brought forth by the popping of the three pronged debt/dollar/bond bubble of which is a mathematical certainty because they cannot be sustained by any means.

OK, so what else to we know?
The DOW/Gold ratio will correct to at least one to one, although I am predicting better than that in favor of gold. So that poses this question: how low is the DOW going to go?
Before I answer that question let's be mindful that the Fed is at some point is going to initiate another form of quantitative easing which will serve once again in creating an even more massive debt/dollar/bond bubble. How big can this get? Frankly who knows, but the bigger

it gets the more punishment is going to be forced upon the general public, and this beating is going to be severe.

The other thing we know is this: as the endgame plays out the Fed is going to be forced to purchase an ever increasing amount of U.S. Treasury bonds simply because countries like China and India who are at this time are the largest purchaser of U.S. Debt, will simply say enough is enough and buy no more.

Understand, the current U.S. bonds being held not just by China and India but all of them in their entirety are not going to be paid back, there is no way America can do it. Therefore the debt is in a massive ultra-bubble which cannot be sustained by any means.

The other factor which the Chinese as well as all the countries which now hold U.S. Treasury bonds are well aware of is this: due to the monetizing of the debt by the Fed any monies which in theory "could" be paid back would be done so with devalued currency. What this means is every single entity, government or otherwise, which now holds a United States Treasury bond is guaranteed to lose money on these said bonds because the Fed has taken purchasing power out of the dollar!

Now at some point in the not so distant future when the debt/dollar/bond bubble pops, whatever the eventual astronomic number may be at that time, **it all becomes PAYMENT DUE IN FULL.** So what happens then? Obviously America does not have the money to pay it back, so default occurs. **Even if Ben were to crank up every printing press he has, and even builds more in an attempt to monetize the debt in total in order to pay our creditors the effect will be the same.**

A worthless or near worthless currency. It is this scenario, a debt default by the United States which is a mathematical certainty that is going to be responsible for and create the gold super bubble I am predicting.

Now all this leads us back to the question I posed earlier which was: how low is the DOW going to go? I will answer that question now.

In 2007 the DOW hit a high of 14,164, much of this was fueled by the housing bubble which allowed our economy to boom beginning sometime in the mid 1980's when the DOW was around 1,500. So we now know that the housing bubble has burst and subsequently the drivers of that bubble are now gone. We now have high unemployment and are continuing in somewhat of a deflationary environment, except for food and energy. The prospects for real economic growth are bleak at best, because without some kind of catalyst to get the economy back on track we are just about dead in the water.

Now if the Federal Reserve would have not intervened with QE1, then QE2, and increasing the monetary base 300% since 2008 all of this would have already corrected to fair market value and at this point in time and although we would still be hurting to some extent, our wounds would have begun to heal.

It is exceedingly difficult to put a number on how low the DOW will go, however we can by taking several factors into the equation guesstimate. We hit a high of around 14,000 in late 2007, and the low since that time was around 6,500 in early 2009, then the Fed stepped in with QE effectively putting a halt to natural market drivers. Consider this, when we had a free market, *something which the Federal Reserve has ended by direct intervention as I have detailed throughout this book,* it was the markets sole job to determine fair market value.

In essence the Fed is telling the investing world as a whole that they know better and subsequently had to step in and save the markets, a very dangerous and portentous thing indeed.

In 2007 when the market peaked the national debt was around ten trillion, it is 33% larger now and growing rapidly. Also at that time the monetary base was over 300% less. In 2009 the national debt grew to around twelve trillion and the Fed had increased the monetary base by the fore mentioned 300%. We now have a national deficit at over fifteen trillion which also exceeds 100% of GDP.

Prior to all this market manipulation by the Fed, a prediction on where the DOW may have bottomed out would have been much easier, and I would say a good guess would have been somewhere around 5,000, but now it is way tougher to make an accurate prediction but I am going to anyway. I would say based on the information at this time a good guesstimate in my opinion would be DOW 4,000. It could go less because of a fear driven over-correction, possibly as low as DOW 3,500, but understand I am making these guesstimates based on the bursting of the three pronged super bubble scenario which I elaborated on at length earlier on.

The other factor which is extremely difficult to factor in to this equation would be the rate of inflation, although HIGH would be a good and simple guess. I realize this is a very stark outlook, believe me, but consider the fact that before the Fed stepped in with QE the DOW had hit 6,500 the economy was in much better shape than it is now and there was no panic selling.

So what does this mean for gold? As I have been saying I sincerely believe that the next super bubble is going to be in gold. I also affirm that the DOW/Gold ratio will correct better that one to one.

I believe we are going to see gold go to 2X the value of the DOW at minimum, so, my prediction for gold is going to be somewhere around $8,000 an ounce, could it go even higher? Sure, but that is my prediction.

What does this mean for crude? Also a massive spike.

I started off this segment with: *Accumulate as much silver as you can possibly get your hands on,*
and here is where the real cheesecake is going to be. Silver is the investment of the century and this is where just about anyone can get in on this game.

Today the spot price of silver is around $32.00 which puts the silver/gold ratio at about 53 to 1. Historically this ratio is 15 to 1, I am sure you can see where I am going with this.

Gold is going to be the next super bubble topping out at around $8,000, of this I have no doubt. If silver were to just attain its historic norm of 15 to 1 we are looking at a spot price of silver of around $500 an ounce however, I believe that this ratio is going to be closer to 10 to 1 before this all plays out and I will tell you why. As we know supply, demand, and human perception are the main market drivers in asset price, I have gone over that at length. Gold and silver are exceedingly rare and as such they are priced accordingly based in U.S. Dollars.

We also know that central banks have been net buyers of gold for the last 3 years, something which has not occurred in decades as central banks are generally net sellers of gold. Countries around the world who have had gold stored here in the United States are now repatriating their gold from the U.S. This reparation of gold by countries around the world from the U.S. is now common knowledge, therefore you can see clearly that they too are preparing for some major future event.

The reason I believe that silver is going to correct better than its historic norm is this, <u>its cheap</u>, much cheaper than gold, and when people get wind of this they are going to sell everything including the kitchen sink rushing to get some. There are going to be supply concerns which I believe will not be able to keep up with demand, and the perception that silver is a "must have" by the general public is going to start a buying frenzy. At this point in time, public perception regarding silver would be 100% correct.
Right now virtually anyone can afford silver as the spot price is about $32.00 an ounce, not so much for gold.

Plus people are not that stupid, and eventually they are going to wake up to the fact that with regard to the silver to gold ratio, silver is more than a bargain which promises to pay off huge when this all plays out.

There are a total of 535 Members of Congress, one hundred serve in the U.S. Senate, while 435 serve in the U.S. House of Representatives, of these 47% are millionaires. Tell me, where do you think they are keeping their money? In cash? Absolutely not. How about big business? They all have massive portfolios and they too are net buyers of gold, although they do have legions of very savvy traders taking both long and short positions on equities, I should know, I used to be one of them.

So now you are aware of where the politicocorporatists, the central banks, and even foreign countries are putting their money. Desplte what the talking heads on the television are saying regarding the price of gold, this is what is driving the price, a limited supply and increasing demand.

At the beginning of this book I began by elaborating on human behavior and perception, how fear and greed often forces an assets price beyond that what fundamental or technical factors would dictate, well here is where that all comes into play. Having an understanding based on historical data in conjunction with the typical behavior of human beings during these times makes it easy to predict the most likely outcomes.

I hope I have convinced you by presenting you with a logical explanation that the next super bubble is going to be gold, however I am suggesting that you buy silver. Earlier on I discussed the current and historic ratios between the two precious metals, currently 53 to 1, historically 15 to 1, what this tells us is that no matter what happens to gold, silver will outperform gold over time. And here is the beauty of it, at this time virtually anyone can afford to exchange some of the Fed's fiat money for real currency, *silver.*

There are several reputable companies which will sell you precious metals, go online, check it out, do a little research into the company's and find the one that is best for you. Precious metals are the easiest thing to not only accumulate but to sell as well. If you choose, all of the companies which sell these metals also buy them. You can also sell them to anyone who may want to buy them from you. I am also going to let you in on a little secret, heck we are friends now right? When you sell your precious metals you do not have to pay capital gains tax. I want you to re-read the previous sentence and focus on these two words, *have* and *to*, you figure out the rest.

Moving on.

What you, me, the politicocorporatists, central banks, and various countries in the world are now waiting for is the gold super bubble, and we are going to take advantage of that by accumulating as much silver as we can get our hands on.

We are going to in essence become our own central banks, we are going to preserve and create wealth for ourselves by accumulating silver.

Right now gold, and especially silver, judging with the knowledge we have now are at fire sale prices beyond a shadow of a doubt.

As the three pronged bubble collapses we are going to witness the largest transfer of wealth the world has ever seen, at the end of this there will only be two classes of people, the upper class and the lower class, *the middle class will be gone.*
Which class do you want to be? Its up to you at this point.

So now that I have outlined the first step of how you and I are going to begin to create wealth, wait, you thought I was done? No no, that's just half the story.

After the endgame.

Let's call this section, overtime.

By this point if you have heeded my advice, that means you would have played your cards just right.

Now what do we do? Simple.

When this gold super bubble has played out, at or near the top of the spike when there is still huge demand for our silver it will then be time to sell our precious metal, a sad time indeed.

You didn't think you were going to keep it forever now did you?

So you have accumulated silver and now the end game in metals is here. Hypothetically, let's say you had acquired 500 troy ounces of silver bullion by this time and the gold super bubble tops out at $7, 654.00 an ounce. Now let's also low ball it and say silver made it just to its historical norm ratio of 15 to 1, (as you know I am predicting 10 to 1), you now have an amount of silver worth $255,133.00

Time to say goodbye to our beautiful shiny metal as this party has ended, the gold super bubble has topped out and we have succeeded in our plan.

What we are going to do at this point is put our newly acquired money into one or more distressed assets which will be abundantly available at that time.

When everybody went scrambling for an exit as their assets value plummeted, that over-correction in the real estate and equity markets had occurred, *and that* is where we want to put our new money to work.

Let's look at the dollar bills symbolism again just for a
moment.

I want you to look at the pyramid for a moment, observe
how the top portion is disconnected from the bottom
section, **these proportions are correct.** After all this is
said and done the ones who aware, the ones on top, are
going to be the winners of this game, and the ones below
moving ever closer to the bottom are going to be the
woeful losers.

America's debt/war based economy.

Before I end this book I thought that it would be important to speak a little more about how our "debt based/war based economy" functions.

As we know since going off the gold standard in 1971 the value of the dollar has been in a downward trajectory, continually sucking more and more purchasing power from every person/country/entity who currently is holding our debt based money. (Holders of the dollar are also those who purchase/hold U.S. treasury bonds or any dollar derivatives).

Before we were taken off the gold standard in a stealthy calculated move between the MIC, OPEC, and the U.S. policymakers, we did not have a debt based economy, what we had was an economy built upon the creation of wealth for the U.S. citizens and our country as a whole, America was truly the land of opportunity.

The Constitution of the United States notes explicitly that all money's created (printed or otherwise) be backed by an equal amount of gold and or silver, in fact there is no amendment to the Constitution which allows for a fiat, or debt based monetary system. Therefore It could be considered that what the Federal Reserve does/is doing by issuing debt as money is "counterfeiting."

Debt based economies which is unfortunately the model for most of the world, is the root cause of the debt problems being faced by the world today, the debt crisis. If we/the world did not have debt based economies none of the problems facing the world with regard to sovereign debt would exist.

Think of it this way, during the gold standard when an individual earned money in reality they were receiving gold, the paper money issued represented the currency which was the gold and silver stored in government stockpiles therefore, during the gold standard the government and the Federal Reserve did not issue debt it issued real wealth.

Today because of our fiat monetary system the only thing which is issued by the Federal Reserve in the form of fake fiat counterfeit money is debt. Each bill/coin issued represents debt owed back to the Federal Reserve plus any accrued interest. The central banks of the world all work in the same manner, they issue public debt which creates private wealth for themselves.

What the Federal Reserve does is criminal plain and simple. The Fed literally prints money out of thin air and then distributes that created money backed by nothing which is then owed back to them with any accrued interest in the form of debt.

The Federal Reserve is the biggest counterfeiter on the Earth.

It is also the Fed who is responsible for the three pronged debt/dollar/bond mega bubble we are in right now, something I have elaborated on at length in the text.

The entire fiat monetary system of the United States was created for one purpose in collusion between the worlds central bankers and the Military Industrial Complex, and that purpose is **WAR**.

I have elaborated on several occasions in this book the real reasons why we were taken off the gold standard, it is a very simple and straightforward concept. The central bankers/Federal Reserve in direct collusion with the Military Industrial Complex wanted to create a fiat monetary system and there reasons were twofold: first, a fiat monetary system would allow the Federal Reserve to now create mass public debt while at the same time creating mass private wealth for themselves, wealth beyond imagination. Think about it for a moment, every dollar held by all of America's people, rich and poor alike, as well as every government backed bond/dollar derivative etc. etc is actually owned by the Federal Reserve. So every dollar in existence is "owned" and "owed back" to the Federal Reserve plus interest. Now that is incredible, don't you think?

The second reason for the creation of a fiat monetary system is so there would be a literal endless supply of money available to fight any and all wars the MIC would choose to fight then, (the Vietnam war), and any other war in in the future.

So each dollar in your pocket or bank account is an IOU, made payable directly to the Federal Reserve plus interest.

It must be understood that the business of WAR is the single largest generator of monies on the Earth, the cost of war in dollars is staggering. In fact the sole reason why the dollar is now the worlds reserve currency, as discussed in the text, is the OPEC nations agreed to price their oil in U.S. dollars in exchange for military protection of that said oil, (the petrodollar accord).

The true reason why we fought the Vietnam war was to first establish a fiat monetary system and second, to create the petrodollar system. Do you think it was just coincidence that we went off the gold standard at the same time the petrodollar system was created? And we went off the gold standard to finance the Vietnam war.

Think about this for a moment, if America was not involved in some type of military conflict many of America's biggest corporations would not exist. These companies which create weapons of war such as Boeing, Lockheed Martin, Grumman, General Dynamics, etc. etc., (there are thousands of corporations spanning the globe which supply and create high tech weaponry, aircraft, ships, munitions, and all manner of war sustaining/fighting equipment) and all of them have a vested interest in the generation and expansion of war. It is also no secret that all these corporations are major contributors to America's policymakers to the tune of tens of billions or dollars. For our policymakers it is their interests, *the interests of the corporations especially the ones which sustain war which are important*, not those of you or I.

My Grandfather used to say "money talks and shit walks," and it took me a long time to figure out what that meant but I think I got it now.

Every war fought by the United States after WWII has been one of choice, not necessity.

Of all the nations on the Earth the United States has the largest global military presence, and America also holds the record with regard to the amount of military campaigns fought by any civilized nation, do you now understand why?

Our current debt based economy is designed to create debtors, not wealth, and war, not peace.

Financial stability or indentured servants?
Very briefly, who are the IMF (International Monetary Fund) and the World Bank?
In 1944 in what was known as the Bretton Woods agreement the IMF and World Bank were created. These institutions are complex and I will not elaborate on how they are structured however, their mission is stated as to foster global financial stability, monitor global economies as to not allow situations to be created which could possibly lead to monetary dysfunction as in the stock market crash of 1929.

Their mission also includes offering loans to already impoverished nations and financial assistance, also in the form of loans to nations requiring it. So what they try to do is solve debt problems by adding more debt, just like the Federal Reserve does, as well as the European Central Bank is trying to do in Europe right now.

With a show of hands how many of you believe you can solve a debt problem by adding more debt!?

OK, so the BIS, IMF, World Bank, ECB and the Fed all have the same mission, and that is to again foster financial stability globally-In this mission they all have failed miserably, that is if you actually believe that is their mission.

All of these institutions are creators of debt and debtors, not wealth. Their sole job is to enslave the world through and with debt. Understand, each of these institutions are privately owned and they are not non-profit. These organizations, (cartel), serve to create profit for those individuals which own them, basically private banks.

Each of these organizations is responsible for the galactic global debt crisis we are now in the midst of, and it is also they who are acquiring gold in mass as of late. Does this seem strange to you? The very organizations which create mass public debt on a global scale are now net buyers of gold.

As I have stated several times in this book, these entities are very well aware that the global debt issues/crisis cannot be fixed by any means, and it is also they who are continuing to inflate the gargantuan debt bubbles of not just the United States but the world.

If you retain anything from this book let it be this: a popping of the three pronged debt bubble which we have gone over at length in this book is a mathematical certainty, and it is deliberately continuing to be fueled with purpose: **to bring about the greatest transfer of wealth the world has ever seen**-And I want you to be on the winning side.

The End.

Notes.

.

Made in the USA
Lexington, KY
11 May 2012